How to Win in Small Claims Court in New York

HOW TO WIN IN SMALL CLAIMS COURT IN NEW YORK

with forms

———

James L. Rogers
Mark Warda
Attorneys at Law

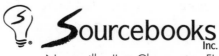

Sourcebooks
Inc.
Naperville, IL • Clearwater, FL

Published by: **Sourcebooks, Inc.**

Naperville Office
P.O. Box 372
Naperville, Illinois 60566
(630) 961-3900
Fax: 630-961-2168

Clearwater Office
P.O. Box 25
Clearwater, Florida 33757
(813) 587-0999
Fax: 813-586-5088

Cover Design: Andrew Sardina/Dominique Raccah, Sourcebooks, Inc.
Interior Design and Production: Andrew Sardina, Sourcebooks, Inc.

This publication is designed to provide accurate and authoritative information in regard to the subject matter covered. It is sold with the understanding that the publisher is not engaged in rendering legal, accounting, or other professional service. If legal advice or other expert assistance is required, the services of a competent professional person should be sought.
From a Declaration of Principles Jointly Adopted by a Committee of the American Bar Association and a Committee of Publishers and Associations

Library of Congress Cataloging-in-Publication Data
Rogers, James L.
    How to win in small claims court in New York : with forms / James
L. Rogers, Mark Warda.
      p.   cm.
    Includes index.
    ISBN 1-57071-187-9 (pbk.)
    1. Small claims courts—New York (State)—popular works. 2. Small
claims courts—New York (State—Forms.   I. Warda, Mark.
II. Title.
KFN5976.Z9R64   1997
347.747'04—dc21
                                                                 97-37047
                                                                    CIP

Printed and bound in the United States of America.
Paperback — 10 9 8 7 6 5 4 3 2 1

CONTENTS

Using Self-Help
Law Books

Whenever you shop for a product or service, you encounter various levels of quality and price. In deciding what product or service to buy, you make a cost/value analysis on the basis of your willingness to pay and the quality you desire.

When buying a car, you decide whether you want transportation, comfort, status, or sex appeal. Accordingly, you decide among such choices as a Neon, a Lincoln, a Rolls Royce, or a Porsche. Before making a decision, you usually weigh the merits of each option against the cost.

When you get a headache, you can take a pain reliever (such as aspirin) or visit a medical specialist for a neurological examination. Given this choice, most people, of course, take a pain reliever, since it costs only pennies, whereas a medical examination costs hundreds of dollars and takes a lot of time. This is usually a logical choice because rarely is anything more than a pain reliever needed for a headache. But in some cases, a headache may indicate a brain tumor, and failing to see a specialist right away can result in complications. Should everyone with a headache go to a specialist? Of course not, but people treating their own illnesses must realize that they are betting on the basis of their cost/value analysis of the situation, they are taking the most logical option.

The same cost/value analysis must be made in deciding to do one's own legal work. Many legal situations are very straight forward, requiring a simple form and no complicated analysis. Anyone with a little intelligence and a book of instructions can handle the matter without outside help.

But there is always the chance that complications are involved that only an attorney would notice. To simplify the law into a book like this, several legal cases often must be condensed into a single sentence or paragraph. Otherwise, the book would be several hundred pages long and too complicated for most people. However, this simplification necessarily leaves out many details and nuances that would apply to special or unusual situations. Also, there are many ways to interpret most legal questions. Your case may come before a judge who disagrees with the analysis of our authors.

Therefore, in deciding to use a self-help law book and to do your own legal work, you must realize that you are making a cost/value analysis and deciding that the chance your case will not turn out to your satisfaction is outweighed by the money you will save in doing it yourself. Most people handling their own simple legal matters never have a problem, but occasionally people find that it ended up costing them more to have an attorney straighten out the situation than it would have if they had hired an attorney in the beginning. Keep this in mind while handling your case, and be sure to consult an attorney if you feel you might need further guidance.

INTRODUCTION

New York's small claims court system provides a useful procedure for collecting small debts. Many claims are too small to warrant the services of an attorney, but too big to ignore.

Simply filing a small claims case often gets results from people who know they owe money but haven't gotten around to paying it. Being brought before a judge is not something people look forward to, and sometimes delivery of a summons brings an immediate check. On the other hand, going through the whole case and winning a judgment may be useless. If a person has no money, there is nothing for you to collect.

While the small claims court was designed to make it possible to take court action without the expense of an attorney, legal advice can be very valuable in determining whether or not to sue, or deciding what claims or defenses to present. If you do not have an attorney, you can probably get an initial consultation for a very reasonable fee through the New York Lawyer Referral Service at (800) 342-6661.

Before filing your case it is advisable to read this entire text. Sometimes information relating to the end of the process is important in planning the beginning, or a decision made in the beginning may affect the procedures in the end.

INTRODUCTION TO SMALL CLAIMS COURT

1

WHAT IS SMALL CLAIMS COURT?

Small claims court is a simple, informal, and inexpensive procedure for the prompt determination of a claim in accordance with basic legal principles. The parties do not need to be represented by a lawyer, and the rules of procedure are simplified so that the technical rules usually used in court are not applied.

Persons winning a case in small claims court are granted a *judgment*. This is a court order stating that they are entitled to a sum of money. In some cases the judgment is not worth anything, for example when the other person has no money with which to pay it. But with persistence money can often be collected on a judgment. A judgment can be good for twenty years as a lien on any property owned by the person it is made against. (See chapter 8, COLLECTING YOUR JUDGMENT.)

WHAT TYPES OF CASES CAN BE HEARD?

Small claims court is used to collect small sums of money. As of the date of publication of this book the limit in small claims court is $3,000. You should check with your court clerk to see if the limit has been changed.

If your claim is for more than the limit of small claims court you may still use small claims court if you are willing to accept an amount up to the limit. For example, if someone owes you $3,500 you may want to sue in small claims court and be happy with a judgment for $3,000. This would be better than hiring a lawyer to sue for the whole $3,500 in a regular part of the court since his or her fees would probably be more than the $500 you would have to forego in small claims court. If you sue for a debt greater than the limit, the defendant may ask that your case be thrown out because it exceeds the limit. Therefore, you should make clear in your court papers or to the judge at the hearing that you wish to waive all amounts over the limit.

Another possibility is to divide your claim into several suits, each of which is under the limit. For example, if you loaned someone $2000 on two different occasions, you could probably treat each loan as a separate transaction and file two suits for $2000 each. However, if you gave him one check for $4000 you could probably not break it into two suits just to get into small claims court. The person you are suing may try to have the suits combined in order to lower the amount of the possible judgment, so you should be prepared to explain to the judge why the matters are separate transactions.

Do You Need an Attorney?

If your case is simple and you have the time to do the work yourself, you probably don't need an attorney. Small claims court was designed for people who do not plan to use and attorney. But if the issues are complicated, you may wish to at least consult with an attorney for advice in handling your case. Some attorneys will provide advice at an hourly rate without actually handling the case in court.

In most cases, each party must pay his or her own attorney's fees, no matter who wins. But in some cases, such as where a written contract allows attorney's fees, the loser must pay the winner's attorney's fees. If your case is like this, then it is important to get the advice of an attorney before filling your case especially if the other side is expected to have an attorney. Otherwise, a simple mistake on your part may result in the other side winning the case plus attorney's fees.

Any time the other side hired an attorney you should consider consulting one. Although the judges are supposed to be flexible in the rules, and some judges side with the party who is not represented, a good lawyer may help avoid fatal flaws in your case.

If you consult an attorney on your case, you might be able to get the other side to pay your attorney fees. The loser can be required to pay attorney fees if there is a written contract that says so. The other side will probably argue that since the attorney did not appear in court you are not entitled to fees, but you should argue that you did consult an attorney concerning the case and kept the fees down by not having the lawyer spend unnecessary time in court. Be sure to have a bill from the lawyer to present to the judge.

WHERE ELSE CAN YOU GET HELP?

The court clerks are supposed to help you prepare the necessary statement to start your case, as well as assist you with enforcing your claim should you obtain a judgment and the defendant refuses to pay you.

You should *always listen carefully to the advice of the clerk*. If he or she says that something is important in your case, don't assume you have a better idea unless you are sure the law says otherwise. Although most court clerks are not attorneys, they will have gained a lot of practical legal knowledge through their employment and will often know the procedures that you must follow inside and out.

The majority of the law that the court follows in small claims cases is contained in appendix A of this book. If you have any questions about how a procedure works, you should check these rules. These laws can often be found in the legal section of your library. In some instances, you may have to go to a law library such as at a law school to obtain these references.

WHAT CAN YOU RECOVER?

As a general rule, you can only recover actual out-of-pocket losses *directly* relating to the subject matter of the suit. For example, if you are suing a cleaners for ruining a dress or an auto mechanic for improperly repairing your car, you can sue for the value of the dress or for the cost of proper repairs. You can't recover for the fact that you missed a job interview or party because you didn't have the dress or car. Nor can you recover lost wages for time you spend in court or your travel costs to court, even if you had to fly in from out-of-state.

In a personal injury case there may be more damages related to the accident. For example, in a car accident you may have medical bills, lost pay from missing work, damage to your car, and pain and suffering.

If you are the *prevailing party*, meaning you won on a significant issue in the case, then you may be awarded your *costs* of the suit. These include your filing fee, sheriff's fee and witness fees. Therefore, if you have a good case, it might be worth spending $100 in costs to win a $50 case because you would be entitled to $150 if you win.

As discussed in the next chapter, you should ask for as much as possible within the small claims court limit in order to improve your negotiating position (even if you know you will not be granted everything in court), but as a practical matter, you usually won't get much more than out-of-pocket losses.

TERMINOLOGY

The following terms are used in small claims court and should be understood by the parties.

Alias Service—a second attempt to serve papers on a party.

Answer—a paper filed by a party in response to a legal pleading.

Claimant—the person who is asserting a legal right in court. Generally, the claimant is the plaintiff. However, if the defendant files a counter-claim, the defendant may also be referred to as a claimant.

Commercial Claim—a money action brought by a corporation, partnership or association which has its principal office in New York state in the commercial claims part of the court. The maximum amount of such claim is equivalent to the maximum amount which can be brought in the small claims part.

Compensatory Damages—damages awarded to restore a plaintiff to the position he or she was in before a wrong was committed.

Consumer Transaction—a transaction where the money, property or service which is the subject of the transaction is used primarily for personal, family or household purposes.

Counter-Defendant—when the defendant files a counterclaim, the plaintiff in the original suit is the counter-defendant in the counterclaim.

Counter-Plaintiff—when the defendant files a counterclaim, he is the counter-plaintiff in the counterclaim.

Counterclaim—when a defendant countersues a plaintiff, he files a counterclaim.

Crossclaim—when there are two or more defendants and one defendant sues another defendant in the same suit, he files a crossclaim against the other defendant.

Defendant—person defending against a claim.

Motion—a request for a court to do something.

Plaintiff—person filing a claim.

Pluries Service—a third or subsequent attempt to serve papers on a person.

Punitive Damages—damages awarded to a plaintiff in order to punish a defendant and restrain a defendant from committing the similar wrongs in the future.

Replevin—a suit for return of property.

Service of Process—the act of handing court papers to a party in the case.

Subpoena Duces Tecum—a document issued by the court ordering a person to bring something to a hearing.

Subpoena—a document issue by the court ordering a person to appear at a hearing.

Summons—a court document informing someone of a court action.

Third Party Defendant—when a defendant wants to bring another party into the suit   that party is the third party defendant.

BEFORE YOU SUE

SHOULD YOU SUE?

Before you file a case in any court you should first analyze whether it is worth your time and effort to go through the whole process. You want to file a case because you are upset about something, but it will be even more upsetting if you lose. Especially if you end up paying damages to the other side. Most cases settle out of court because you can never predict what result you will get in court. No matter how right you are, or how strong you case is, the court can rule the other way for any number of reasons.

DO YOU HAVE A CASE?

In order to win a lawsuit against someone, you must be able to prove they are liable under some acceptable legal theory. In many instances, a person who has clearly suffered a loss may not be able to win their case because the law doesn't place the liability on another person. Before filing your case you must find a legal theory which will allow you to collect. Some cases are easy. If a person did something intentionally (like break your window) or failed to do something which was legally required (like pay back a loan) then you have a clear case.

But in other cases you must use a more complicated theory, such as negligence or implied warranty. In cases like these you will only win if the facts of your case fit into the legal definitions of negligence or implied warranty. If you are struck by lightning while walking at Disney World, the owners will probably not be liable because the courts consider lightning an "act of God" and not the legal responsibility of the landowner. (A person once tried to sue God for an act of God. He served the papers on a local church as an "agent of God." But the court said that the church was not legally able to accept service of process for God so the court "did not have jurisdiction over the defendant.")

For another example, imagine you have rented a house from a landlord. When you signed the lease you agreed to take care of minor maintenance and the landlord agreed to charge you less rent. Now suppose you fixed a board on the steps and later it broke and you fell, breaking your leg. Even though the landlord owns the property and has insurance against liability, he will probably not have to pay for your broken leg because you had the duty to maintain the premises and you are the one who improperly fixed the step which broke.

If you signed a contract or received any papers from the other party relating to the transaction, you should read them before filing suit. Sometimes they will limit your legal rights or your right to bring suit. If a business made promises about a product but the contract said the product was sold "as is" and that "oral representations cannot be relied upon," you may be out of luck. Or if your contract with your stock broker says that you agree to arbitration, you may have given up your right to sue.

In some cases, the papers used by the party may not have any legal effect. A lease may say that a landlord is not liable for injuries on the premises, but in some instances New York law says otherwise and this overrules the wording of the lease. A ticket you receive when bringing an item for repair may say that the repair shop is not liable if the item is lost or destroyed, but New York law may allow you to recover anyway.

If you have any doubts about your rights you should check with an attorney or do some research yourself. Many types of claims are explained in this book, but if you are industrious you may want to do some extra legal research to find other grounds for your suit. You can do legal research at the law library found in most county courthouses or in many law schools. There are also several books on the market explaining how to do legal research. If you cannot find one locally, contact Sourcebooks, Inc. at (800) 226-5291.

CAN YOU PROVE YOUR CASE?

Even if you have a good case, you will not win if you do not have enough proof to convince the judge that you are right. If all you have is a verbal agreement, it will be your word against the defendant's and the judge will have to decide who is more believable. If you do not have any evidence and the other side has evidence which supports his side of the case, you will be less likely to win.

Be sure to read the rules of evidence in chapter 8. Also, ask your friends what they see as the best points of the other side's case. As a participant in the situation, you will not be able to effectively judge the other side's arguments. Your friends may provide an objective opinion. If there is a chance you will be countersued, you should consider consulting with an attorney. He or she may be able to point out a legal rule or other reason that you could lose the case.

IS IT WORTH YOUR TIME AND EFFORT?

Even if you have a legal claim, not all claims are worth bringing to court. Sometimes it may cost you more to take off work for two hearings than the claim is worth. If there is a chance you will be countersued then you are risking more than just your time and effort.

Of course, in many cases the principle is more important than the money and you may enjoy the process of getting justice from someone who took advantage of you. But be sure to consider what the case will involve before you start it.

You should also consider that it might not be worth the time and effort for the other side to fight your case. If the amount involved is small and they will have to take off work or hire an attorney, they may just settle with you without a trial. So merely filing the case may get results.

CAN YOU COLLECT IF YOU WIN?

If the person you want to sue has no money, it may be a waste of time to got to court. In New York, a large amount of a debtor's property is exempt from creditor's claims. So a judgment you spent time and court costs to obtain, may end up being a worthless piece of paper. (See chapter 8, COLLECTING YOUR JUDGMENT for more information on exempt property of a judgment debtor.)

The best party to sue is a large corporation or a person with a lot of real estate or other assets. (You can check the property records in the courthouse and the state motor vehicle records to see what a person owns.) If you have a valid claim, a large corporation will probably pay you rather than spend the money to defend itself. If you are suing a person who owns real estate, your judgment can be placed as a lien on all of their holdings for up to twenty years.

The worst parties to sue are small corporations with no assets or people who have no assets and are supporting a family.

If you are not sure if the party is worth suing, you might want to read chapter 8 in this book before filing your claim. It explains how to find out what a person's assets are.

Caution! You should not sue anyone unless you have a valid claim. If you file a suit and the judge decides there is really no legal or factual merit to it, he or she may place a judgment against *you* for all of the other party's attorney's fees and court costs.

WHAT SHOULD YOU DO BEFORE FILING YOUR SUIT?

Before filing your suit you should attempt to work it out with the other person. People sometimes come to court and say they haven't paid an amount owed because they were never asked. Even if you have asked the person to settle the matter, you should send at least one letter and keep a copy of it. This can be used as evidence in court that you have tried to resolve the matter.

In some counties there are mediation or arbitration services. If you think it might help, you should contact them before filing your suit and try to work something out with the other party.

When negotiating to settle a case you should be sure not to let the time limit pass for filing your case. There is a law called the statute of limitations which gives time limitations as to when each type of suit can be filed. Once the deadline has passed, the claim is forever barred and may not be sued upon. For example, for a suit against a physician for medical malpractice the limit is two years and six months, but for a suit against a municipality such as a city, county, town, or village the limit is one year and ninety days. For other types of suits see chapter 4.

If the limitations deadline is near and the person you are negotiating with seems to be delaying, you may have to file your suit to avoid missing the deadline. One way to avoid the deadline without filing suit is to have the person sign a promissory note. This is considered a new agreement and the limitation period is six years from the date the final payment is due.

Filing Your Case 3

Who Can Sue?

INDIVIDUALS

You, as an individual, may use the small claims court to recover money which you believe someone owes you. Remember that the most money you can sue for in small claims court is $3,000.

No one can use the small claims court as a means to harass another person. The clerk of the court has the discretion to compel anyone which the court believes may be using the court for such a purpose to make a special application to the court for a determination as to whether the claim can be brought. The circumstances warranting such an application might be where a person has previously brought the same suit with an adverse judgment.

PARTNERSHIPS AND ASSOCIATIONS

A partnership or an association can not sue in the small claims part of the court. However, partnerships and associations can sue for the maximum amount permitted for a small claim ($3,000) in the commercial claims part of the appropriate court. No partnership or association can bring more than five such commercial claims per month.

The rules for commercial claims are very similar to the rules for small claims. Thus all the rules in this book apply to commercial claims brought by partnerships and associations. Where differences exist, these differences are stated.

CORPORATIONS With the exception of nonprofit corporations, a corporation can not sue in the small claims part of the court. However, a corporation which has its principle office in New York state can sue for the maximum amount permitted for a small claim ($3,000) in the commercial claims part of the court. A corporation is limited to bringing five such commercial claims per month.

The rules for commercial claims are very similar to the rules for small claims and where differences exist in this book, these differences are stated.

A corporation may appear as a party in a commercial claim action by any authorized officer, director or employee of the corporation who has the requisite authority to bind the corporation in a settlement or trial. In the alternative, the corporation may appear by an attorney.

TRUSTEES AND FIDUCIARIES Trustees and fiduciaries such as personal representatives of estates or guardians may sue as long as they properly identify their capacity.

INFANTS AND INCOMPETENTS Infants, defined as persons under the age of eighteen, must sue through a proper representative such as a parent having legal custody or a guardian of the infant's property unless the court appoints what is called a *guardian ad litem*. A person who has been judicially declared incompetent must appear in court by the conservator of such a person's property.

MULTIPLE PARTIES Persons who assert any right to relief jointly, severally or in the alternative arising out of the same transaction, occurrence or series of transactions or occurrences may join in one action as plaintiffs if any question of law or fact would arise. This means that if you and another person suffered damages as the result of a common action by the defendant, you may join with this other person in one action against the defendant. However, given the monetary limit on small claim actions

($3,000), you would probably be better off to bring your own action separately if your own claim is near the $3,000 limit.

COUNTIES, CITIES, TOWNS AND VILLAGES

You can bring a lawsuit against a county, city, town, or village in small claims court. However, if your claim is for the negligence of such a county, city, town or village (also called a *public corporation*), you must serve what is called a *notice of claim* within ninety days from the time that the negligent act occurs. If you do not file this notice of claim, your suit may be barred. Service of a notice of claim has been held by some courts not to be merely a procedural matter which can be waived under the relaxed evidentiary and pleading rules of the small claims part but is rather a rule of substantive law that you must follow.

Your notice of claim must be in writing, sworn to by or on behalf of you, and it must set forth your name, address, the nature of your claim, the time when, the place where and the manner in which you claim arose. You must also set forth the items of damage or injuries you are claiming to the extent possible.

You must serve your notice of claim upon the county, city, town, or village you plan to sue by either delivering it personally or by sending it by registered or certified mail to the appropriate person designated to receive such service. Generally, the safest way to insure that you have served this notice on the proper person is to serve it upon the attorney who represents such county, city, town or village although there are other options to you under the Civil Procedure Law and Rules depending on the type of public corporation you want to sue.

A form which you can tailor for your notice of claim appears in appendix B. If you want more information on a notice of claim, see General Municipal Law §50-(e)(I).

Whom Do You Sue?

It is important to sue the correct party or your judgment may be worthless. Even worse, you may have to pay for a person's attorney's fee if you sue him or her without good legal grounds.

INDIVIDUALS   Be sure to get the exact name of the party you are suing. Don't sue "Mr. & Mrs. Smith." You need to have the correct spelling of their full names. If you don't know their middle names it is not crucial, but the more precise you are the better.

SPOUSES   Whenever you have legal grounds, you should sue both spouses. If you get a judgment against just one person and he or she owns property with a spouse, you may not be able to put a lien on it or seize it. But a judgment against both a husband and wife can be filed as a lien against all of the property owned by either or both of them. Whenever you have a plausible legal reason to sue a spouse, do it. For example, if you are trying to collect back rent from a tenant, even if only one party usually paid the rent, you could argue that both were tenants and one was the agent of the other.

MINORS AND INCOMPETENTS   You cannot sue a person under eighteen years of age or an incompetent person unless you also sue his guardian or have one appointed by the court. For an injury caused by a minor, you could in most cases sue his natural parents. Having a guardian appointed by the court would require the services of an attorney.

CORPORATIONS   A corporation with assets is a good target, but a "shell" corporation with no assets is not. It can be dissolved, making your claim worthless. An individual may have no assets or may file bankruptcy, but it is not as likely or as easy as dissolving a shell corporation. A new corporation can always be started, but an individual is stuck with his credit record for years.

In such a case, it is better if you can sue some of the individuals in the corporation. This can be done if the individuals signed documents without their corporate titles, or if the company name was used without the words "Inc.," "Corp.," or "Co." after it, or if the individuals committed some sort of fraud. It can also be done where a corporation has been undercapitalized and in a few other circumstances.

Ignoring a corporate entity and suing the individuals behind it is called "piercing the corporate veil" and much has been written about it in legal books and periodicals. If you think you will need to pierce a corporate veil to win your case you should research the subject further in your nearest law library.

PARTNERSHIPS   You cannot sue a partnership as such, you must sue the individuals who are the partners. If you do not know who the partners are, you should read the following section. For a limited partnership you need only sue the general partners. However, your judgment will only be against assets of the partnership and the general partners. The personal assets of the limited partners are not subject to claims against the partnership.

FICTITIOUS   You can't sue a "company" unless it is a corporation. If it is a sole pro-
NAMES   prietorship or a partnership, you must name the individuals and add "d/b/a" (doing business as) and then the company name. For example you might sue:

John Smith d/b/a Smith Company, or

John Smith, Raymond Smith and William Smith

d/b/a Smith Enterprises, a partnership

If you don't know who the principals of the business are, you can look them up. Under New York's General Business Law (§130), no person may conduct a business in New York under any name other than his or her real name, unless he or she files a certificate in the office of the clerk of each county in which the business is conducted. Any person who knowingly fails to comply with this law is guilty of a misdemeanor and will be prohibited from bringing any lawsuit on any contract made in this fictitious name until a certificate has been filed.

The county clerk's office must maintain an alphabetical index of all filed certificates under the fictitious name. Once you have located the certificate under the fictitious name, you will be able to obtain the true name or names of the person or persons conducting the business as well as the residence address of each such person since this information must be contained in the certificate.

If you still cannot locate the true name of the person or persons who are conducting a business, chances are such person(s) have either failed to file a certificate or you are dealing with a corporation which may be using a fictitious name. Corporations which conduct business under a fictitious name must also file a certificate and face the same consequences if they fail to do so. However, you will only find the fictitious name of a corporation in the Office of the Secretary of State since this is the place where corporations are required by law to file such certificates. For the secretary of state you can call (518) 474-4750 or write to New York Department of State, Divisions of Corporations, 162 Washington Avenue, Albany, New York 12210.

WHERE TO FILE YOUR SUIT

You, as a plaintiff, must sue in the small claims part of a court that is convenient for the defendant. In other words, if the person you want to sue does not live or have an office for business or is not employed near the court that you want to use to file a claim, you will not be able to use that court to sue the defendant. This is a major difference between suing a defendant in small claims court as opposed to the regular part of the court where you might even be able to force a defendant who lives out of the state to defend your suit.

The following rules apply with respect to where you may bring your small claims action:

1. If you want to sue in the New York City Civil Court, the defendant must either reside, or have an office for his or her business or be employed in the city of New York.

2. If you want to sue in a justice court of your village or town, the defendant must either reside, or have an office for his or her business or be employed within that town or village where the justice court is located.

3. If you want to sue in a city court, the defendant must either reside or have an office for his or her business or be employed within the county where the city court is located.

Example: Alison's landlord refused to return her security deposit after she had vacated her apartment according to the terms of her lease. Alison sued her landlord in the small claims part of city court in Albany, New York for $450, the amount of her security deposit. Alison's landlord lived in California and handled his dealings with all of his tenants in New York through a rental agent. Alison's small claim suit was dismissed on the basis that the court had no jurisdiction over the suit since the landlord neither resided, was employed, or maintained an office for business in Albany county.

Perhaps the easiest way to find the small claims court that you may file your claim is to start with your telephone blue pages under the name of your city or town and looks for courts. If you do not find a listing specifically for small claims, you can call any general reference number of a court in your location and usually obtain the number for the small claims court of your locality. Once you have obtained the number and location of your small claims court, you should make sure that the defendant you want to sue meets the above requirements or else you will need to choose a small claims court which is closer to the defendant. As always, the clerk of your small claims court will be helpful in deciding whether the defendant can be sued in the court you have chosen.

WHAT ARE THE FEES?

At the time this book was published, the filing fee in the small claims part was $10 for all small claims under $1,000 and $15 for all small claims over the amount of $1,000. If you are bringing a commercial claims as a corporation, partnership or association, the filling fee is $22.84. Personal checks are not usually accepted.

If you are suing for wages which do not exceed $300 which an employer refuses to pay you either after you have made a written or verbal demand for these wages, you should not have to pay any filing fee. To take advantage of this rule you will have to submit an affidavit to the clerk stating that your claim does not exceed $300, that you have a good and meritorious cause of action against your employer for the wages owed, that you are an employee or resident in the county you are bringing your claim (or the city of New York if you are suing in the civil court of New York city) and that you have made either a written or verbal demand upon the employer for payment of your wages and this payment was refused.

HOW DO YOU BEGIN?

INDIVIDUALS If you are filing in your own name as an individual, you or someone on your behalf should go to the appropriate court to pay the required filing fee to start your case. You will be required to fill out an application for your claim and must provide your name and address, the name and address of the defendant's place of residence, business or employment to do this. You or the person filing the claim on your behalf must then sign the application and will then be provided with the date and time for the small claims hearing. An example of the type of application you must fill out is provided in Form 1 of this book.

Be sure to obtain a pamphlet which your court should have called *A Guide For the Use of the Small Claims Part*. It will contain a lot of valuable information on how to file a small claims court action.

CORPORATIONS,
PARTNERSHIPS, OR
ASSOCIATIONS

If you are bringing a commercial claim on behalf of a corporation, partnership, or association, you must also go to the appropriate commercial part of you court to pay the required filing fee and fill out an application. The commercial part will most likely be located in the same place as the small claims part of the court, and the application will usually be on the same page as for a small claims action. For an example of the type of application used, see Form 1 of this book

The application will contain a certification that no more than five commercial actions have been filed in the month that you are bringing suit. Moreover, if your commercial claim is based on a consumer transaction in that the subject matter over which you are suing was used primarily for personal, family or household purposes, you will also be required to sign a verification that you have mailed to the defendant a demand letter, no less than ten days and no more than 180 days prior to the time that you file your claim. Therefore, if your claim involves such a consumer transaction, you will have to send this demand letter prior to starting your case.

Your demand letter must contain the following information; the date of the consumer transaction that forms the basis for your suit, the amount that remains unpaid, a copy of the original debt instrument or other documents underlying the debt, any accounting of any payments made, and if you were not a party to the original transaction, the names and addresses of the parties to the original transaction. The demand letter must also contain a statement that you intend to use the commercial claims part to obtain a judgment, that further notice of a hearing will be sent, unless payment is received by a specified date, and that the defendant is entitled to appear at the hearing and present any defenses to the claim. You can obtain a form for your demand letter from the court or you may use Form 2 in this book.

Be sure to ask for a pamphlet which your court should have called *A Guide For the Use of the Commercial Claims Part*. It contains a lot of information on how to use the commercial claims part of your court.

POSSIBLE CLAIMS (LAWSUITS) AND WHAT YOU MUST PROVE

While the facts of your claim (lawsuit) will inevitably be unique in that it will involve specific events concerning you, the judge who presides over your case will be looking to see that your case fits under a category of cases for which the law can grant you relief. Moreover, even if you case fits under this category, the judge will require that you prove all of the necessary elements which must be proved for that type of case in order to recover.

While you are not a lawyer and no one at your hearing will expect you to know what the law is regarding your case, you will be more effective in presenting and hopefully winning your case if you have a good idea of what type of case you are bringing and what you must prove in order to win that particular kind of case. (Remember, you will have only a limited amount of time to present you case to the judge.) Knowing whether you can make out all the necessary elements which must be proved to win your case, will also better enable you to determine whether you should consider any settlement offers by a defendant and yes, even whether you should pursue a claim in the first place.

The following is an explanation of the types of suits which are usually brought before small claims court, and the necessary elements of each which you must prove in order to prevail at your hearing. Occasionally, your lawsuit will seem to apply to more than one of the following claims. In such an instance, you should present both claims to the judge rather than mistakenly exclude a different possible claim only to find out later that your case could have been proved using this excluded claim.

ACCOUNT STATED   This is an action to recover money owed on an account where the parties agreed to a balance but the customer never paid. To win an account case, you must prove: a) the parties had previous dealings that were always paid or quickly questioned, b) a statement for the claimed amount was rendered, c) the defendant did not object to the statement which raised a presumption of assent, and d) the defendant never paid. The advantage to this claim over a suit for payment for the goods themselves is that with this claim the other side cannot bring up the quality of the goods as a defense.

It may seem unfair, but by not objecting to an incorrect bill, a person agrees to pay it, and may be legally bound to pay it even if it is wrong. For customers, this means it is important to always question incorrect bills immediately; for businesses, it means it is important to send out regular statements.

Note that all four elements must be present to win this action. If the defendant disproves one of the elements you will lose.

OPEN ACCOUNT   This is an action to recover money owed on an open account, such as when a customer receives goods or services and is rendered a monthly bill. This is easier to collect than to sue for the value of the goods or services because if a person gets several regular bills and does not object to them, they can't contest the value of the goods or services later. To win a suit on an open account you must prove: a) the defendant had a charge account, b) a statement was rendered, c) the amount of the balance, and d) it was never paid.

If you are not sure you can prove all the elements for an open account claim, you might want to file a claim using three different alternate claims, in the expectation that at least one of them will be successful.

GOODS OR SERVICES SOLD   This is an action to recover money owed for goods or services sold. To win a suit for goods or services sold, you must be able to identify the goods or services and prove: a) the defendant purchased them, b) a price was agreed to, and c) the goods or services were never paid for. If no price was agreed to, then you must prove the reasonable value of the goods or services.

GOODS OR
SERVICES SOLD/
ACCOUNT STATED/
OPEN ACCOUNT

If you are not sure if you have the evidence to prove any one of the previous three claims, then you should consider filing a three-count claim. In this claim you alternately claim each of the three grounds for collection. If your evidence is insufficient for one, you still have a chance to prevail under another. Of course, you cannot collect triple the amount of the debt.

IMPROPER
SERVICES

This is an action to recover money that was paid for services which were not performed properly. To win a suit for improper services, unless it is obvious that the service was improper, you must provide an expert witness who can testify the services actually were improper. The expert must be someone trained in the field of those services who examined the matter in the suit. For example, if a new roof leaked shortly after it was installed, it would probably be obvious that it was improperly done. But if you feel your car was not working properly after it was serviced, you would need another mechanic to testify that the repairs were done incorrectly.

PROMISSORY
NOTE

This is an action to recover money owed on a promissory note which has not been paid on maturity. To win a suit on a note, you must prove: a) the defendant executed the note, b) it is past due, c) demand for payment was made, and d) it was not paid.

UNPAID RENT

This is an action to recover rent from a tenant. To collect unpaid rent you must prove: a) there was a written or oral agreement to pay a sum of rent and b) the defendant breached the agreement by failing to pay.

This is not an eviction action. It is only for collection of money and is usually used to collect unpaid rent after the tenant has left. To evict a tenant you must commence a summary proceeding. A summary proceeding may be commenced in a County Court, the Court of a Police Justice of a village, a Justice Court, a court of civil jurisdiction in a city, or a District Court. For eviction forms and instructions see *Landlords'*

Rights and Duties in New York, by Paul W. Barnard and Mark Warda, also published by Sourcebooks, Inc.

DAMAGES TO PREMISES
This is an action by a landlord to recover money for damage to rental premises and may include a claim for unpaid rent. To collect for damage to premises, you must prove that the damages were done by the tenant or during the tenant's term of occupancy. This means you must have witnesses who saw the premises before and after the tenant took possession. Photographs are very useful to a judge in such a case. Normal wear and tear is not considered damages, so if you have to repaint the property or clean the carpeting after a tenant has lived there several years, that would be normal expenses of being a landlord and not the tenant's liability.

Like the claim for unpaid rent, this is not an eviction action. See the explanation under UNPAID RENT on page 28.

SECURITY DEPOSIT
This is an action by a tenant to recover a security deposit which was kept by a landlord. Upon the expiration of the time of your lease, you have a cause of action for the return of your security deposit which has been wrongfully withheld by your landlord. Where you have given money to your landlord as security for the faithful performance of all your obligations under the lease, you are entitled to the return of the deposited money except to the extent that the landlord can show that he or she has been damaged by a breach of some promise which you made in the lease.

BAD CHECK
This is an action to collect on a check that was worthless because of in sufficient funds or any other reason. After you have received a worthless check, you should present it to a bank and have them mark on it the reason it was not paid. Then, you should send a Bad Check Notice by certified mail, return receipt requested, to the person who wrote the check.

You should be aware that it is a misdemeanor for any person to issue a bad check knowing that he or she does not have sufficient funds in a bank to cover the check.

BREACH OF CONTRACT	This is an action to recover money damages for failure of a party to abide by the terms of an oral or written contract. To win a suit for breach of contract you must prove: a) there was a written or oral agreement between the parties, b) the defendant did not perform or performed improperly, and c) you performed or were ready, willing and able to perform your part of the agreement.
AUTO ACCIDENT	This is an action to recover money for damages sustained in an automobile accident. To win a claim for damages from an automobile accident, you must be able to prove: a) the defendant caused some damage, and b) it was done negligently (or intentionally). To prove negligence you can use a guilty plea as evidence, but you can't use a conviction of a traffic violation. (The reason people plead *nolo contendere* is that it is not a guilty plea which could be used against them). However, you can use the same witnesses as in the traffic case, and if you can prove the other party violated a traffic law, that would usually be proof of negligence.
ASSAULT AND BATTERY	An *assault* is an attempt, displayed by violence or threatening gesture, to do injury to or commit a battery on another person. A *battery* is the actual wrongful physical contact with the person of another without the consent of the victim. In addition to compensatory damages such as any medical bills or loss of earnings which occurs as a result of an assault and battery, you may be awarded *punitive* damages to punish the defendant. Although there are defenses to an assault and battery such as "self-defense," no provocative act or word, if unaccompanied by an overt act of hostility will justify an assault or battery no matter how offensive it may be. Provocative remarks, however, may be considered in the lessening of damages in a proper case.
BREACH OF EXPRESS WARRANTY	This is a claim for damages when a product or service does not live up to an expressly worded warranty. To win such a case, a person must prove: a) there really was a warranty given (written or oral), b) the product or service breached the warranty, and c) some damages resulted from the breach.

BREACH OF IMPLIED WARRANTY

One good catch-all claim is for implied warranty. This is a claim used when a product or service does not fulfill its basic purpose. The three types of implied warranties are:

Warranty of Title. If you were sold an item that the seller didn't own and that you had to return to the rightful owner (such as stolen property), you could sue the seller for breach of the implied warranty that he had title to the property he sold you. To do so you must prove: a) you paid for the item, and b) you did not obtain title to it.

Warranty of Merchantability. When goods are sold by a dealer in such merchandise, unless they are sold "as is," there is an implied warranty that they are fit for the purpose for which they are made. If a washing machine does not wash, it is not merchantable. If bread is moldy, it is not merchantable. To win a claim for breach of the warranty of merchantability, you must prove that the goods were not merchantable when received. If, for example, a car broke down two weeks after it was purchased, you could not collect for breach of such a warranty unless you could prove that at the time of the sale the car was in such a condition as to make it unmerchantable. If a part was ready to break, you would probably win. If it broke because you hit a bad bump in the road, you would probably lose.

Warranty of Fitness for a Particular Purpose. When a seller represents himself as being knowledgeable about a product and sells it to a person for a known particular purpose, there is an implied warranty of fitness for that purpose. For example, if a body building gym sells a piece of pipe for use as a weight lifting bar and it bends, there would a breach of a warranty even if it was a perfectly good pipe for other purposes. To win a suit for an implied warranty, you need to prove that the seller was knowledgeable about both the product and your reason for needing it, and that the product was not proper for your purpose.

LEMON LAW

New York has two "Lemon Laws" which you should consult if you are the purchaser of an automobile. The new car lemon law is found at General Business Law §198-a and the used car lemon law is found at

General Business Law §198B. Unfortunately, these statutes are quite lengthy and complex. But you should consult them directly because they contain important information about things that you must do in order to preserve your rights under these statutes. If you see that your dealer has violated a provision of the statute, then you should point this out to your dealer.

With the expense of new automobiles reaching prices of over $20,000, you most likely will not bring an action in small claims court for the return of your purchase price. Remember, that the maximum amount of money that a small claims court can hear is $3,000. Also, you can only sue for money damages in a small claims court whereas the remedy you may really seek is simply a replacement by the dealer of your defective automobile. In such cases, you will be required to hire an attorney and bring your case in the regular part of a court.

POSSIBLE DEFENSES

Before you file a case you should consider whether the defendant has any valid defenses or a counterclaim against you. You should review chapter 4 of this book to see if your claim would be barred by some legal rule. Consider any claims a defendant might be able to make against you. Occasionally, a person filing a small claim ends up losing a lot more than he was suing for.

DISCLOSURE

Disclosure is the term used when one party (the *moving party*) asks the court to compel the opposing party to make available the information that the moving party needs to prepare for the case. For example, if you are suing the defendant for negligence in performing some type of service for you, it might be helpful to know the particular training background of the defendant before you go into the courtroom. In a regular lawsuit, there are extensive procedures which you could use to compel the defendant to make such information available to you. However, these devices are not normally permitted in a small claims action unless you can demonstrate some special or compelling need for the information. In other words, you can only ask the court to compel a defendant to disclose, prior to trial, information which is absolutely necessary to your ability to present your case at the hearing.

In most cases, there will not be a compelling need for you to obtain disclosure of information prior to the hearing. However, if you feel that the defendant has some type of information which is absolutely necessary to the presentation of your case, you should consult with the clerk of the court about bringing a motion to the court to decide whether you have the right to compel the defendant to provide you this information prior to your hearing.

CAN YOU GET A JURY TRIAL?

You, as a plaintiff (claimant), do not have the right to a jury trial in small claims court. By bringing an action in the small claims part you are deemed to have waived your right to ask for a jury trial. The only possible time that you may have a right to demand a jury trial after starting a small claims action is if your case is removed from the small claim part to a regular part of the court. In that instance, the procedures of the regular court would apply and you would have the right to ask for a jury trial.

Defending Yourself 4

What If You Are Sued?

If you are sued in small claims court, you should read all of the documents carefully to find out where to appear in court and what you are being sued for.

If you know the claim is true, you should contact the other party and try to settle the matter. You should not waste the court's time and incur additional expenses if you know you owe the money you are being sued for. If you don't have the money, you could offer to sign a promissory note to make regular payments or you could sign a stipulation in the court case to make payments.

DO NOT IGNORE A NOTICE OF CLAIM! If you have received a notice of a plaintiff's claim against you informing you of the date and time for a hearing of the case, you may feel for whatever reason that you should simply ignore the date set for your hearing. This is a huge mistake since if you do not show up to your hearing, the plaintiff will in all likelihood be granted a judgment of default against you. Once the plaintiff has obtained his of her judgment of default, the plaintiff has a whole array of methods of going after any of your assets to satisfy this judgment. There have been cases where wealthy individuals have ignored suits which they thought were silly and then lost great amounts of property when the court seized their buildings to pay off judgments as small as $100. If you cannot attend the hearing call the court and ask for an adjournment.

WHAT ARE YOUR DEFENSES?

Before you decide to settle the case you should review your defenses in the matter and see if the claim is legally enforceable. There are many possible defenses to a claim that you (and the plaintiff) may not know about.

Read all of the following possible defenses and see if any of them apply to your case. If you think any might, be sure to mention them to the judge if your case does go to court. Some of the defenses may just delay the case, and if you are in a hurry to get it over with you might not want to use them, even if they do apply. But many of them are defenses that could win the case for you.

IMPROPER NOTICE

The clerk of the court will handle sending you notice of the plaintiff's claim. Notice must be sent by ordinary first class mail and return receipt requested. However, just because the clerk has this duty does not mean that notice does not have to be given to you exactly as the law requires. If you have not been given notice precisely as required under the law, you can raise this fact as a defense to the court's jurisdiction over you.

Under New York law, you must be given notice of the plaintiff's small claim action by ordinary first class mail and by certified mail, return receipt requested. This notice must be sent to your residence. However, if your residence is unknown or you do not reside within the county of the court (if the plaintiff is using a city or justice court) or the city of New York (if the plaintiff is using New York City Civil Court) or within the appropriate district (if the plaintiff is using a district court), then such notice can be given at your office or place of regular employment within the town or village (if plaintiff is using a justice court) or within the county of the city court (if plaintiff is using a city court) or within the city of New York (if plaintiff is using the New York City Civil Court) or within the appropriate district (if plaintiff is using a district court).

If after the expiration of twenty-one days (thirty days for a commercial claim in a city court), the first class mailing has not been returned as undeliverable, you will be presumed to have received notice of the plaintiff's claim. The notice that you must receive must be in substantially the same form as is printed in Form 3 in this book.

EXAMPLE   Megan, who resided out of state, and her sister, Kate, who resided at 21 Beaver street, Buffalo, New York, both owned a house that they rented at 2 Park Place in Buffalo. A visitor of one of their tenants at 2 Park Place sued Megan and Kate in the small claims part of Buffalo city court after the visitor was injured when he tripped and fell while walking through a corridor to the apartments. The clerk of the court sent out two separate notices to 21 Beaver street. One of the notices named Megan as a defendant and the other notice named Kate as a defendant. While the notice addressed to Kate was valid since Kate resided at 21 Beaver street, the notice addressed to Megan was not valid because Megan neither resided, maintained an office or was employed at 21 Beaver street. Megan could properly seek dismissal of the small claims action with respect to herself.

JURISDICTION   If you are not being sued in the proper court, then the court does not have jurisdiction to hear the plaintiff's case. See chapter 3, WHERE TO FILE YOUR SUIT, to make sure that the plaintiff can sue you in the small claims court that the plaintiff has chosen. If the plaintiff is not suing you in a court that has jurisdiction over you, then you should seek dismissal of your case on this ground.

DENIAL   First read the statement of claim and all exhibits carefully to see if everything is true. Look at your records and compare the dates and other details. Perhaps the claim is untrue. If an important aspect of the claim is untrue, you may win the case.

FOREIGN
CORPORATIONS

You may run into a *foreign corporation* which is simply a corporation formed under the laws of another state. Foreign corporations that conduct regular business in New York are required to obtain authorization to do business from the Secretary of State. If your plaintiff is such a corporation, then you should check with the Secretary of State to determine if the corporation has obtained authorization to do business in New York. You can call the Secretary of State in Albany at (518) 474-4750 to check on the corporation's status. You can also write to the Secretary of State and make up to five free inquiries regarding the status of any corporation (the fee is five dollars for each additional inquiry) at the following address:

> New York State Department of State
> Divisions of Corporations
> 41 State Street, 2nd Floor
> Albany, New York 12231

If your foreign corporation does not have authorization to conduct business in New York, it can not maintain an action against you, and you should ask that any lawsuit by the corporation be dismissed on this basis.

FICTITIOUS
NAMES

Any person who conducts a business in New York under any name or designation other than such person's real name, must file a certificate in the office of the clerk of each county in which the business is conducted, or in the case of corporations conducting business under a fictitious name, with the Secretary of State. Any person who fails to do this is prohibited from maintaining any action or proceeding in any court on any contract, account or transaction made in a name other than its real name until the required certificate has been filed. So if your plaintiff conducts business under a fictitious name, then you should check to see that the necessary certificate has been filed. If the certificate is not on file, then you should ask that the plaintiff's case be dismissed on this ground.

RES JUDICATA

Res Judicata is an old legal rule meaning that the case has already been decided. There can only be one case on each single controversy. If a court already considered a matter, a new court cannot reopen it. For example, if you sued a tenant for an eviction under a lease, he can't bring a new case later claiming you violated the lease. He should have brought up the matter as a counterclaim in the original suit.

With respect to the defense of res judicata and small claims judgments, there are some special rules that limit the defense. Any judgment obtained by a party in a small claims action is only res judicata with respect to the amount sued for in that action. For example, if you are a doctor and your patient sues you in small claims court and later wins a judgment for $500, this judgment can only be used by you as a defense for up to the amount of $500 in a subsequent lawsuit by the plaintiff against you. So if the plaintiff's second lawsuit against you is for the amount of $3,000, the most the plaintiff could recover would be $2,500 since you have a res judicata defense for the amount of $500 due to the prior lawsuit for that amount. If the plaintiff's prior lawsuit had been brought in a regular part of the court, then you would have a complete defense for any dollar amount which the plaintiff's tries to seek from you in a subsequent lawsuit.

The limitation of the res judicata defense with respect to prior actions brought in small claims court is based on the principal that small claims actions do not provide litigants all the procedural safeguards of a regular lawsuit and that parties are limited in the dollar amount which they can sue for in the first place. For example, if a party, who has not sought legal counsel, has a huge malpractice suit and unknowingly decides to sue for a small dollar amount in a small claims court, it is thought that a judgment in small claims court for that small dollar amount should not limit that plaintiff beyond that dollar amount recovered if he or she later does realize that the amount they could have recovered was substantially greater than he or she thought. Unfortunately, this limits your ability as a defendant to use the res judicata defense.

LACK OF CONSIDERATION

Promises to make gifts are not enforceable. Therefore, if you signed a promise to pay someone and never received anything in return, the promise would be unenforceable. This can be used in many kinds of cases. For example, if you promised to give your neighbors your old car when you got a new one, they could not win a suit for the car if you changed your mind, since they didn't do anything for the car. However, if you told them you would give them your old car if they mowed your lawn every week, and they did mow your lawn, then they could sue you and win.

As another example, if you agreed to pay $1000 for a diamond ring and signed a promissory note to the seller, then discovered the stone to be glass, you could probably avoid paying the note because you got nothing for it. (You could probably also use the fraud or the mutual mistake defenses.) However, if you borrowed the money from a third party such as a bank, you could probably not avoid repaying the bank for the loan because the bank is not responsible for the condition of the item you bought.

Also, if you bought something and signed a promissory note and then the dealer sold the note to a bank or other lender, you could probably not avoid paying the note, since the bank would be considered an innocent buyer of the note and the law encourages the easy sale of "commercial paper." Many businesses that sell questionable products quickly sell the loan papers so that the buyers cannot stop payment. Sometimes the bank or other lender can lose the case if they are part of a conspiracy with the business, but this type of case would be difficult to prove.

STATUTE OF FRAUDS

Certain agreements are not enforceable if they are not in writing. Even if the facts are true and money is owed, the law says that these agreements just won't be enforced by the court if they are not written and signed. The writing need not be a formal contract. Canceled checks and short memoranda signed by one party have, in some cases, been held to be sufficient. The following are instances when the agreement must be in writing. For further research, the relevant statute citations from the General Obligations Law and Uniform Commercial Code are included with each.

☞ Sales or transfers of any interest in real estate (Gen Oblig Law §5-703(1,2)).

☞ Leases for a period longer than one year (Gen Oblig Law §5-703(2)).

☞ Guarantees of debts of another person (Gen Oblig Law §5-701(a)(2)).

☞ Sales of goods over $500 (UCC §2-201).

☞ Agreements which take longer than one year to complete (Gen Oblig Law §5-701(a)(1)).

☞ Sales of securities (UCC §8-319).

☞ Agreements made in consideration of marriage, except mutual promises to marry (Gen Oblig Law §5-701(a)(3)).

☞ A subsequent or new promise to pay a debt discharged in bankruptcy (Gen Oblig Law §5- 701(5)).

☞ Assignment of a life, death or accident insurance policy or the promise to name a beneficiary of any such policy. (Gen Oblig Law §5-701(9)).

☞ The promise of a grantee (a person to whom real estate is conveyed) to pay off a mortgage on the real estate which existed prior to the conveyance. (Gen Oblig Law §5-705).

MINORS An agreement entered into by a minor is generally not enforceable in court. The exceptions to this are if the minor continues to fulfill the agreement after reaching majority or if the agreement was for a "necessity." Thus, if a minor signed an agreement to buy a car, it would probably not be enforceable, but if he signed a check to pay for food it probably would be.

PAYMENT If you have actually paid the money claimed to be owed, this would be a defense to the claim. Perhaps the money was credited to a wrong account or not credited at all. To prevail with this defense you should have some evidence that you have made payment, such as a cancelled check or a receipt.

ACCORD AND SATISFACTION

If a debt is in dispute and the parties agree to a settlement, such as acceptance of fifty percent of the debt, this should finally settle the matter. If one party later claims the whole amount in a suit, the settlement agreement would be a defense. This agreement of accord and satisfaction should, of course, be in writing, but even if it is not, it may be enforceable.

PAYMENT AFTER SUIT IS FILED

Once a suit is filed, the loser will usually have to pay the court costs in addition to the money owed. This usually consists of the filing fee and the sheriff's fee. If the amount owed is in dispute, the defendant can pay what he thinks he owes into the registry of the court and if the judgment is not for a greater amount, he won't have to pay the court costs.

STATUTE OF LIMITATIONS

The laws of every state give time limits on how long claims can be brought. After a certain time, claims will not be allowed by the court, no matter how valid they are. Thus, if a person waits too long to file a suit, his or her claim may not be enforceable. These time limits on when an action must be commenced are called *statutes of limitations*. Usually the time limitations begin to run from the day that you committed the act which the plaintiff is complaining about. However, there are a few exceptions to this general rule.

Listed below are various actions and their respective time limitations that each action must be commenced. Also listed is the statute section from the Civil Practice Procedure Law and Rules, the General Obligation Law and the Uniform Commercial Code where you can find the particular limitation for further research.

The following actions must be commenced within twenty years:

☞ Actions to collect on a money judgment. (CPLR §211(b).)

☞ Actions to enforce any temporary or permanent order or judgment which awards support, alimony or maintenance. (CPLR §211(e).)

The following actions must be commenced within six years:

☞ Actions based on a contract, except with respect to contracts for the sales of goods. (CPLR §213(2).)

☞ Actions upon a bond or a note secured by a mortgage upon real property or actions upon a mortgage of real property. (CPLR §213(4).)

The following actions must be commenced within four years:

☞ Contracts for the sale of goods. (UCC §2-725.)

The following actions must be commence within three years:

☞ Actions to recover damages for a personal injury, generally. (CPLR §214(5).)

☞ Actions to recover for malpractice, other than for medical, dental or podiatric malpractice. (CPLR §214(6).)

☞ Actions to recover damages for injury to one's property, generally. (CPLR §214(4).)

☞ Actions based on fraud or mistake. (CPLR §213(6,8).)

☞ Actions to recover a chattel or for damages due to the taking or detaining of a chattel. (CPLR §214(3).)

The following actions must be commenced within two years and six months:

☞ Actions for medical, dental or podiatric malpractice, except were the action is based upon the discovery of a foreign object in the body of the patient in which case the time limitation is one year from the date of discovery or from the date of discovery of facts which would reasonably lead to such discovery whichever is earlier. (CPLR §214(a).)

The following actions must be commenced within one year and ninety days:

☞ Actions against municipalities such a city, county, town or village. (Gen Mun Law §50-I.)

The following actions must be commenced within one year.

☞ Actions upon an arbitration award. (CPLR §215(5).)

☞ Actions for libel or slander. (CPLR §215(3).)

After reading through the above types of actions and their respective time limitations, if the plaintiff's claim has not been commenced within a respective time period, raise this as a defense to the plaintiff's claim at your hearing.

FRAUD OR MISREPRESENTATION

If you were defrauded in a transaction, or if important facts were misrepresented to you, you may have a valid defense. For example, if you bought a car and later found out the odometer was set back, you can use that as a defense if you are sued for the price of the car. Usually though, such claims should be used for a counterclaim. (See chapter 6.)

MISTAKE OR ERROR

If both parties were mistaken about an agreement they entered into, it can usually be voided. For example, if both parties believed a gem to be a diamond, but it turned out to be a fake, then a sale of it could be rescinded. If only the seller knew it was a fake, this defense would not work, but the fraud defense might.

BREACH OF CONTRACT

If the plaintiff did not fulfill his side of an agreement, he may not be able to sue you to collect on it. Thus, if improper goods were delivered, the seller should not be able to collect. Explain to the judge any ways that the plaintiff failed to fulfill his side of the agreement.

USURY

If you were loaned money at an annual interest rate of over sixteen percent, there may have been a violation of the usury laws. If a bank charges interest in excess of the amount permitted by statute, you (individuals, not corporations) have a defense to the payment of the entire interest on the loan; however, you would still be required to pay back the principal of the loan. For more information on New York's Usury laws, see New York's Banking Law §108 and General Obligations law §§501 et seq.

SALES OF GOODS

Sales of goods are governed by a set of laws called the Uniform Commercial Code (New York statutes Article 2). If you are being sued over a transaction involving a sale of goods there might be some rule that covers your case. For example, if you sold defective goods and the buyer did not give you proper notice that they were defective then he may not be able to win a suit against you.

BANKRUPTCY

If a person files liquidation bankruptcy, the debts listed can be wiped out and completely discharged forever. If a person files a bankruptcy petition while a case is pending, all actions against the person and his property must stop. If you are the plaintiff and a defendant tells you that he has filed bankruptcy, you should call the local federal bankruptcy court to confirm that it has been filed. If you take any action after you have been informed of a bankruptcy then you may be held in contempt of federal court.

In a reorganization bankruptcy, the debts will not be wiped out but the court will approve a schedule for payment of them. Still, you may not take any actions against the debtor while he or she is in bankruptcy.

SETTLING THE CASE

Whether or not you have any defenses to the case, it is usually better to negotiate a settlement than to take a chance with a judge's decision. No matter how sure you are of your case, you can easily lose if your witness doesn't show up or if the other side is more believable, or if any number of things go wrong.

It is often better to take only a partial victory than to risk complete defeat. If the plaintiff understands that he may never be able to collect his judgment, he might accept fifty cents or even twenty-five cents on the dollar for a cash settlement.

Even if you know you owe the full amount, you should try to avoid a judgment being issued against you. This will be damaging to your credit rating. The best arrangement for both sides is to enter into a *Stipulation to Stay Entry of Judgment*. This is an agreement by which the parties agree that if the defendant makes payments according to a certain schedule, no judgment will be entered. It is important for the defendant to keep payment by the schedule or else the judgment will be quickly filed. If the payments are made, no judgment will ever be filed.

Some counties have dispute settlement programs where parties can talk to a mediator and avoid the trouble of court. But such mediation is not binding, and a person who does not get his way may go to court anyway.

SHOULD YOU ASK FOR A JURY TRIAL?

You, as a defendant, have the right to demand a jury trial as long as you make this demand prior to the date set for the hearing of your small claims case. In reality, however, very few small claims defendants demand a jury trial. The reasons are simple; you incur a jury fee expense and up to $25 in costs may also be awarded the plaintiff out of a $50 undertaking that you must post should the plaintiff prevail in the case.

Sometimes defendants use a jury trial demand to make the plaintiff's case more time consuming and complex with the hope of discouraging the plaintiff from pursuing his or her claim. However, this is not really a good strategy because the mere demand for a jury trial does not in itself mean that the case will now turn into a regular lawsuit. The small claims case will remain a small claims case with no additional complexity other than the fact that a jury and not a judge will decide your case based upon the evidence heard.

To demand a jury trial, you must complete a demand letter for a jury trial as well as an attached affidavit stating that your demand is made in good faith and specifying the issues of fact in the plaintiff's action which require a jury trial. A form and affidavit that you can use to make this demand is contained in appendix B.

Issues of fact pertain to facts or events of the plaintiff's case which you and the plaintiff disagree upon. For example, if the plaintiff claims that you were negligent in repairing plaintiff's car, an issue of fact might be whether your repair work was actually the cause of the damage plaintiff is complaining about, or whether you were negligent in repairing the plaintiff's car. Since both of these issues are necessary for plaintiff to prevail, these issues should be enough for you to obtain a jury trial if you want one. To decide what to write on your demand for a jury trial as issues of fact, you should scan the types of actions which a plaintiff to a lawsuit could bring in chapter 3. Once you have found the type of lawsuit that the plaintiff is bringing against you, you should look for the elements that the plaintiff must prove to win such a case. Any event or issue of fact relating to the proof of any of those elements should support your demand for a jury trial.

After completing your jury demand and affidavit, you must file the forms with the clerk of the small claims court. After the clerk receives these forms and you pay all necessary fees, the clerk will transfer the small claims case to the part of the court used for jury trials.

COUNTERSUING 5

THE BEST DEFENSE

The best defense is a good offense, so the best way to defend yourself is to find a reason to sue the plaintiff. If there is only a suit pending against you, the plaintiff will be eager to try the case because he can either win or not win. But if you file a suit against him, he may lose! When both parties have claims against each other, the cases are often dropped or settled quickly because neither party wants to take a chance of losing.

HOW TO COUNTERSUE

You have the right to file a counterclaim against the plaintiff so long as your counterclaim is for money only and does not exceed the dollar amount allowed in small claims actions which was $3,000 at the time this book was published.

You must file any counterclaim you have within five days after receiving notice of the plaintiff's claim. You do this by filing with the clerk of the small claims court a statement containing your counterclaim. You will also be required to pay an applicable filing fee of $3 plus the cost of mailing your counterclaim to the plaintiff. After you have filed your counterclaim, the clerk will send notice of your counterclaim by ordinary first class mail to the plaintiff.

If you fail to file your counterclaim within the five days of your notice of plaintiff's claim, you do not loose your right to file a counterclaim, but the plaintiff (claimant) has the right to request and obtain an adjournment of your scheduled hearing to a latter date. A judge will also have the right to adjourn your case if you wait until trial to bringing up any counterclaims that you may have.

You should review the types of claims that a plaintiff may bring in chapter 3 to see if you have any possible counterclaims against the plaintiff. If you want to sue the plaintiff for more than $3,000 you must bring the suit as a separate action in a regular part of the court.

EXCEEDING THE LIMIT

If you have a claim which is over $3,000, it cannot be heard in small claims court. You will be required to file your claim in a regular part of the court as a separate action which will normally entail the expense of hiring a lawyer due to the much stricter rules of procedure which must be followed.

If your claim is for over $3,000, but you wouldn't mind limiting your judgment to $3,000, you can continue the action in small claims court.

IMPLEADING ADDITIONAL DEFENDANTS

If, after a claim is filed with the clerk, you desire to implead (sue) one or more additional defendants, the clerk will issue and mail, upon receipt of the proper fees, a notice of claim to each additional defendant you want to add. Notice will be given in the same manner as with the original defendant.

The right to implead additional defendants is a right shared by both the plaintiff and the defendant. For example, if you are being sued in a matter and there is someone else involved who has some or all of the responsibility, then you should implead them.

YOUR TRIAL (HEARING) 6

SHOULD YOU AGREE TO ARBITRATION?

There is a good possibility that both parties to a small claims court action will be asked whether they want to submit their case to be heard by an arbitrator rather than a judge of the small claims court. You may even be asked this question after you show up to your scheduled trial. Arbitration is looked upon favorably by the court since it is a means for the court to quickly move cases.

When you agree to arbitration, you normally agree to be bound by the arbitrators decision regardless of the outcome. Thus on the possible negative side of agreeing to arbitration, you should realize that you give up your right to make any appeal of the decision. However, given the limited nature of such a right, this may not sound as important as it seems. The important thing for you to remember is that You are not required to agree to arbitration, and your rejection of arbitration should not have the slightest effect on how the judge of the small claims court decides your case. However, you may be asked to come back to the court at a latter date for your trial if you do not agree to arbitration.

If you agree to arbitration, your arbitrator will be an attorney appointed by the court and will have all the necessary qualifications to decide your case according to the law. In some cases, your arbitrator could even be a judge on the bench or even a retired judge with considerable court decision experience. Each witness who testifies before the arbitrator will be sworn in just like a trial before a small claims judge, and the hearing procedure will be similar if not exactly like it would be if you were appearing before a small claims judge.

The arbitrator will make his or her award in writing and file this with the clerk of the small claims part. Unless both parties file a request not to enter judgment, the clerk will, within two days after this filing, enter judgment in accordance with the arbitrators award.

SHOULD YOU SETTLE BEFORE TRIAL?

Most lawyers will agree it is much better to settle a case and get most of what you want than to hold out for everything and have a trial. Even the most iron-clad cases have been lost at trial. There are many reasons for this. The judge may not believe you, your witness may get the facts mixed up, the judge may feel sorry for the other side, or there may be a little known legal rule precluding your recovery.

If you can come out ahead by settling for part of what you want, you should consider that option. If a tenant offers you $100 in back rent, but you feel he owes $400, you might be better off with $100 in cash than with a $400 judgment you may never collect. Weigh the chances of winning and the chances of actually collecting (and the time involved) with the amount the defendant is willing to settle for and decide if it's worth it.

WILL THERE BE A JURY TRIAL?

As stated previously, a plaintiff is deemed to have waived the right to a jury trial by bringing an action in small claims court. However, any other party to the action may demand a jury trial. (See chapter 4,

SHOULD YOU ASK FOR A JURY TRIAL, for an explanation of a party's right, such as the defendant to ask for a jury trial.

WHAT WILL HAPPEN AT TRIAL?

If you have not settled the case and if the defendant has not defaulted (failed to show up), then a trial will be held. The purpose of the trial is for the judge or jury to hear both sides of the case and decide who should win and what money, if any, is owed.

The trial is your only chance to present your case to the court. You cannot tell the judge that you are not ready or you forgot some of the evidence unless you have some sort of real emergency. If there is an emergency and you must leave town or your witness is unavailable, then you should immediately contact the judge or the court clerk. If you explain the situation to the judge's secretary or the clerk, it may be possible to delay the trial.

Different judges require differing degrees of formality in trial procedure. Some may follow a formal procedure while others may just informally ask each party for his or her side of the case. If the court follows formal procedure the trial will progress as follows:

1. Opening remarks by the judge,

2. Plaintiff's opening statement,

3. Defendant's opening statement,

4. Plaintiff's evidence,

5. Defendant's evidence,

6. Plaintiff's rebuttal and closing argument,

7. Defendant's closing argument,

8. Plaintiff's rebuttal to closing argument, and

9. Judge's decision.

Sometimes the judge does not make a decision in court, but waits a few days and mails out an opinion. There are reasons for this. Sometimes the judge wants to carefully examine or review the evidence or the case law. Other times the judge wants to give the parties time to calm down or wants to avoid a scene in the courtroom.

PREPARATION FOR TRIAL

You should prepare your case so you can present it quickly and in an orderly manner. Review the possible claims and what you must prove for each type of claim contained in chapter 3. You should be sure that you have some proof for each element of your claim in order to win your lawsuit based on that claim.

You should be sure your witnesses will be available (see next chapter) and be sure you know what their testimony will be. If they don't have a good memory of the facts, you may not want them to come to the trial.

PRESENTING YOUR CASE

While the rules of law are the basis for all court decisions, there are certain other factors which must be considered. An unshaven biker in court against an eighty-year-old widow in a wheelchair might have a hard time proving he is an innocent victim.

Appearance is important. Many judges consider shorts or tattered jeans disrespectful of the court system and might be prejudiced against a party because of such attire. On the other hand, if someone dresses too well and wears too much heavy gold jewelry, there might also be prejudice against that person.

One of the most important parts of the case other than the facts themselves is your attitude in court. If you sound sincere and are respectful to the judge, he or she will have more sympathy for your case than if you are rude and make it clear that you won't pay even if you lose.

While you should be prepared for court, you should not bring prepared statements to be read. Make a list of the important points which you plan to cover and refer to your list to be sure that you do not miss any of them.

Pay attention to the judge's questions and answer them directly. If the judge doesn't seem to understand, ask him or her if you should explain. Don't ramble on about meaningless points. Don't say that everyone knows the defendant is a crook. Just explain the facts of your case. Listen carefully to what the judge is asking. It is often an important legal question that will decide the outcome of your case. If you don't understand the question, ask him or her to explain it.

Don't interrupt the other party and don't moan if they are lying. Be polite and wait for your turn to explain or to cross-examine them. While the other side is testifying you should take notes. If the other side lies about something or says something that needs to be explained, write it down. When the other side is done testifying, you will have a chance to cross-examine. At this point you can bring up statement inconsistencies.

The cross-examination is not the time to tell your side of the case. You must ask the other party questions. You should ask them questions that show flaws in their argument. Some examples: If they say you could never clean their pool right, ask them if they continuously used your services for five years. If they say they never borrowed the money from you, ask them why they were sending you checks every month.

Only ask questions that will make them look bad. If they say you never made any repairs in the apartment, don't ask them what items you didn't fix—they'll make a long list and you will only look worse. Ask them, "Didn't I fix the faucet in April? Didn't I fix the roof in June?"

Whatever you do, don't lie under oath. It is a criminal offense. If the other side lies, explain it to the judge when it is your turn to testify. If you explain your side truthfully, it will probably be more believable anyway.

Use your witnesses to verify your side of the facts. Ask the witnesses questions which will lead to answers verifying your side of the facts. Tell the witness ahead of time to be brief and to only answer the questions asked of him. Tell him not to go into long stories unless asked to. If you have five witnesses to the same facts, ask the judge if he wants to hear all of them. If the defendant has no witnesses and you have five, the judge may only want to hear one or two, or may only have a single question for the other witnesses. Sometimes a judge will tell you the other witnesses will not be necessary. Other times the judge will be noncommittal and say it's up to you. In the latter situation, your best bet would be to bring all of the witnesses in, but just ask each witness one or two key questions. If you waste a lot of time or make the judge miss lunch, he or she won't feel very kindly toward your view of the facts.

OTHER THINGS YOU SHOULD REMEMBER DURING YOUR HEARING

If your claim involves the conduct of the defendant's business you should call to the attention of your judge that New York law (§1804 of the various Court Acts) provides the judge or arbitrator must determine the appropriate state or local licensing or certifying authority and any business or professional association of which the defendant is a member. Your claim will involve the conduct of the defendant's business if, for example, you are suing over property that the defendant sold to you and selling this property is the defendant's business. This information could become important to you in respect to enforcement of your judgment since most defendants will be concerned about your notification to any such authority that the defendant refuses to pay for a judgment that you have obtained. But for you to notify any such professional association you need to know about them! Now is a good time to ask the judge to compel the defendant to disclose this information!

Rules of Evidence 7

With a few exceptions, evidentiary rules which apply in a lawsuit brought in a regular part of a court do not apply to small claims actions. This is a good thing for the average layperson since such rules could easily fill up this entire book!

While you will not have to worry about knowing about all the rules which lawyers must consider when making objections during a regular trial, you still must consider what type of evidence you will need in order to convince the judge that you should win your case.

Prima Facie Evidence

New York law states that an itemized bill or invoice receipted or marked paid, or two itemized estimates for services or repairs are admissible in evidence and are *prima facie* evidence of the reasonable value and necessity of such services and repairs. *Prima facie* is a Latin term which translates to "at first sight" but means "presumed true." This rule of law is important and you should pay careful attention to it in order to win your small claims case. The rule is like a rule which says that if the parking meter official writes down that he or she placed a parking ticket on your car, this means (is prima facie evidence) that the ticket was affixed unless you can prove otherwise. Similarly, if you come to court with an itemized bill for services or repairs or you have two itemized estimates for such services or repairs, then you have proved the reasonable value of these services or repairs and their necessity unless your opponent can prove otherwise.

While cases have still been won without a plaintiff bringing to court an itemized bill marked paid or two itemized estimates in a lawsuit seeking damages for services or repairs made, the chances of winning such a case without this evidence are greatly reduced.

WITNESSES

Parties can be their own witnesses, but disinterested witnesses are better. Before bringing a witness to court, be sure to find out what the witness will say. If there are several witnesses, you want to have the best witness for your side of the case.

To be sure a witness will appear in the court, you can subpoena him or her. You can also use what is called a *Subpoena Duces Tecum* to compel a witness to bring some piece of evidence to your hearing. However, you should realize that if people don't want to miss work, and you subpoena them, they may not be your best witness.

Some people, such as relatives or employees, will come at your request and do not have to be subpoenaed. But if you ask someone to come to court and they don't show up, the trial will go on without their testimony. If you have any doubts that your witnesses will show up, you should subpoena them.

To require witnesses to appear in court, you must pay them a witness fee, which is currently fifteen dollars. There is also a fee for mileage, which is currently twenty-three cents per mile to and from the courthouse from the place that you serve your witness. However, no mileage fee is required is your witness is doing all of their traveling within the boundaries of a city. For a person who is not a witness to the incident, but who is an expert, you will have to pay them an expert witness fee. This can be whatever they wish to charge (see below).

The clerk of the court should be able to assist you with preparing a subpoena and is listed as an authorized person who can issue a subpoena without a court order. The clerk may have forms which you can use as a subpoena or you can use the forms which appear in appendix B. The subpoena is served, upon the person named in your subpoena, in the same manner as a summons which generally means that you should personally serve the subpoena upon the individual named in the subpoena. Personal service is completed by having someone who is eighteen years or older, who is not a party to your lawsuit, personally deliver the subpoena to the person named. Your server should also complete an affidavit of service and file this affidavit with the clerk after making the service.

Expert Witnesses

In some cases, it is important to have an expert witness. When trying to prove some work was done wrong, it is best to have an expert testify that he examined the work and it was done wrong.

For example, if you are sued for not paying for an air-conditioning repair and you feel the repairman never got it working right, you should bring in another repairman who examined the unit. If you say you fixed it yourself, or your brother-in-law says it wasn't putting out cold air, it won't be as convincing as if you bring in a repairman with twenty years experience who says it obviously did not have enough freon and that he fixed it.

You may have to pay an expert to investigate your claim and to appear in court. An expert witness does not have to accept the standard fifteen dollar witness fee, but can charge whatever he thinks he is worth. Some experts charge hundreds of dollars per hour. You should check with a few possible expert witnesses before deciding whom to hire. To cut down the expense of having an expert travel to court, ask the judge if he or she may testify by telephone.

PRIVILEGED COMMUNICATIONS

ATTORNEY-CLIENT

One exception to the rule that evidentiary rules of a regular lawsuit do not apply to a small claims hearing is with respect to statutory provisions relating to privileged communications. One of the most well known statutory privileged communications relates to anything which is said between a client and his or her attorney. Unless a client somehow waives this privilege, an attorney is not allowed to disclose nor can the attorney be compelled to disclose any confidential communication made with his or her client during the course of legal representation. Moreover, no employee nor any other person who obtains, without the knowledge of the client, evidence of a confidential communication between an attorney and his or her client can disclose or be compelled to disclose such communication.

It is unlikely, that you will need to invoke your attorney client privilege in small claims court, but if you are ever asked for information that you may have told your attorney, you can invoke this privilege and prevent the required disclosure of such information.

DOCTOR-PATIENT

A second privileged communication which is probably not as well known as the attorney client privilege is any confidential communication made between a patient and his or her physician, dentist, podiatrist, chiropractor or nurse. Unless such a patient waives this privilege, no person who is authorized to practice medicine, who is a registered nurse or licensed to practice dentistry, podiatry or chiropractic medicine can disclose any information obtained in attending to the patient in such a professional capacity. The applicability of this privilege also applies to a medical corporation, a professional service corporation organized to practice medicine, and a university facility practice corporation.

The privilege between applicable medical personnel and a patient can have broad implications. Not only can such a privilege be invoked in court to prevent testimony of such a privilege, but lawsuits have also been brought against physicians for a breach of this privilege.

Testimony Concerning Deceased or Mentally Ill

A second and final exception to the general rule that evidentiary rules of a suit brought in the regular part of a court do not apply to the small claims part relates to testimony concerning a personal transaction or communication with a deceased or mentally ill person. Under New York law, a party to the lawsuit or other interested person may not be examined as a witness in his or her own behalf or interest concerning a personal transaction or communication between the witness and the deceased person or mentally ill person. However, such a party or interested person is not incompetent and thus can testify as to facts of an accident where the proceeding, hearing, defense or cause of action involves a claim of negligence or contributory negligence and where one or more parties is the representative of a deceased or incompetent person based or by reason of the operation or ownership or a motor vehicle being operated on New York highways.

You will most likely never have a need to use this evidentiary rule in small claims court. The rule is most often invoked in will cases where an interested person such as a beneficiary wants to testify as to what a decedent said in respect to the decedent's will.

Proof

In criminal law a defendant must be guilty *beyond a reasonable doubt.* That is a strong burden to overcome. But in civil court a party need only prove his case by a *preponderance of the evidence*, which means anything over 50% (even 50.0001%). The judge will look at the evidence for each side and will see whose evidence is greater and decide the case accordingly, even if there is some doubt.

COLLECTING YOUR JUDGMENT

FIRST STEPS

Once you have won your case, you are only half way to recovery. Next, you must try to collect on your judgment. A judgment is only a finding by the court that money is owed. A person cannot be put in jail for not paying a judgment. Unfortunately for plaintiffs, debtors' prison has been abolished. The only thing you can do if a person does not pay a judgment is to look for his or her property and have the sheriff seize it. If a person has no property, your judgment may be worthless. To look for property which may be available for seizure, you should check the following:

1. The Department of Assessment and Taxation in your town or city for real estate owned by the defendant. (Check other town or city departments if you think they own property elsewhere.) You can search for real estate either under the name of the defendant or you can search the address of a particular property to see if the defendant owns that property.

2. To find information on vehicles which the defendant owns you can obtain from your local New York State Department of Motor Vehicles a form entitled "Request for driver and/or vehicle record information." By providing the name of the defendant or plate

number and class of vehicle owned by the defendant, you can find out the defendant's current vehicle information and if you know the vehicle identification number on a vehicle, you can find out the current owner, plate number and lien information on that vehicle. After completing the form, you mail your request to:

New York State Department of Motor Vehicles

Division of Duty Preparation

Empire State Plaza

Albany, New York 12228-0430

The current fee is five dollars for each search requested.

INFORMATION SUBPOENAS

If your judgment remains unsatisfied, you may serve what is called an *information subpoena* upon any person or upon an officer, director, agent or an employee of a corporation, partnership or sole proprietorship. An information subpoena is simply a list of questions pertaining to the judgment debtor's current or future property. This subpoena is a useful device that you can use to find exactly what your judgment debtor owns so that you can take steps to collect your judgement from such assets.

The person you choose to serve your information subpoena must answer your questions separately and fully under oath and return these answers within six days after receiving your questions. If this person fails to do this, you can seek to have the small claims court hold this person in contempt of court.

The clerk of the small claims court can help you with preparing an information subpoena and may have a form that you can use. One type of form that you can use as an information subpoena appears in appendix B. You must serve your information subpoena along with one copy of it by registered or certified mail, return receipt requested. You must also include a prepaid (i.e. stamped) return envelope addressed to your-self.

RIGHT TO OBTAIN CONSUMER CREDIT REPORTS

A consumer reporting agency can, under New York General Business Law Section 380-b, furnish to an inquiring judgment creditor information in connection with collection of an account of a judgment debtor. This credit report could provide you with another means of obtaining information bearing on your debtor's assets.

EXEMPT PROPERTY

Not all property of a debtor may be seized. Before taking action to seize a defendant's property you must understand what property is exempt under New York law. Here are just some of the property which is exempt from satisfaction of your money judgment.

REAL PROPERTY
The following real property, not exceeding $10,000 in value above liens and encumbrances, owned and occupied as a principle residence by the judgment debtor, is exempt from application to the satisfaction of a money judgment, unless the judgment was recovered wholly for the purchase price of such real property: 1) A lot of land with a dwelling on the land, 2) Shares of stock in a cooperative apartment corporation, 3) Units of a condominium apartment or 4) A mobile home.

PERSONAL PROPERTY
The following are a few of the types of personal property which is exempt from application to the satisfaction of a money judgment except where the judgment is for the purchase price of the exempt property or was recovered by a domestic, laboring person or mechanic for work performed by that person in such capacity: all wearing apparel, household furniture, one mechanical, gas or electric refrigerator, one radio receiver, one television set, crockery, tableware and cooking

utensils necessary for the judgment debtor and the family; necessary working tools and implements, including those of a mechanic, farm machinery, team, professional instruments, furniture, and library, not exceeding six hundred dollars in value which are necessary to the carrying on of the judgment debtor's profession.

TRUST PROPERTY
All property held in trust for a judgment debtor, where the trust has been created by, or the fund so held in trust has proceeded from a person other than the judgment debtor, is exempt from application to the satisfaction of a money judgment. This exemption applies to all trusts, custodial accounts, annuities, insurance contracts, monies, assets or interests established as part of, and all payments from, either any trust or plan, which is qualified as an individual retirement account even though such judgment debtor is an individual who is the depositor to such account plan.

SECURITY DEPOSITS
Money deposited as security for the rental of real property to be used as the residence of the judgment debtor or the judgment debtor's family is exempt from application to the satisfaction of a money judgment.

DOCKETING YOUR JUDGMENT

After your judgment has been entered you should take steps to docket your judgment with the county clerk. You do this by simply requesting a transcript of your judgment from your small claims court and then filing that transcript with the county clerk's office in the county in which your judgment was rendered.

Docketing your judgment means that the county clerk will record your judgment under the name of the defendant in so called docket books. Once you docket your judgment, the judgment becomes a lien, for a period of ten years, on all real property which the defendant owns in that county. If the defendant subsequently transfers his or her property, your lien will continue to remain on the real property.

If you know that the defendant owns real property in some other county besides the county in which your judgment was made, you can also docket your judgment in that county to perfect a lien on that real property. But you must always first docket your judgment in the county in which your judgment was rendered before docketing your judgment in any other county.

Besides creating a lien against the defendant's real property located in the county in which you have docketed your judgment, docketing your judgment gives you another significant advantage in that your judgment will subsequently be given the status of a supreme court judgment; you will now be able to issue executions out of the supreme court giving you statewide enforcement powers to satisfy your judgment.

PROPERTY EXECUTION

A *property execution* is simply a form to an appropriate enforcement officer, usually a sheriff, directing that enforcement officer to levy or sell any non-exempt property which the defendant has an interest in order to pay off your judgment. The execution is required to contain certain information such as the date the judgment was rendered, the court in which it was rendered, the amount of the judgment and the names of the parties. An execution must also state that only the property in which a named judgment debtor who is not deceased has an interest, or the debts owed to the named judgment debtor be levied on or sold and must specify the last known address of the judgment debtor. You will also be required to identify and locate the defendant's property in the execution.

An execution is issued either from the clerk of the court or your attorney as officer of the particular court you are using to issue the execution. If you have docketed your judgment with the county clerk (see prior section on DOCKETING YOUR JUDGMENT,) you can issue your execution using the supreme court. This has an advantage in that the execution will be enforceable against both real and personal property of the defendant throughout New York state.

You can also issue your execution using the court which heard your small claims case but you will be restricted to levying only against personal property of the defendant. If you choose to use the court which heard your small claims case, you will also be restricted as to the geographical area in which you can levy the defendant's property. For example, if you issue your execution through the clerk of your town, village or city court, you can only levy against personal property of the defendant which is located in the county where your court is located. If you issue your execution using the New York City Civil Court, your judgment can only be levied on personal property of the defendant located in the city of New York.

INCOME EXECUTION

If your judgment debtor is employed and earns more than $127.50 per week disposable income, you can file an income execution (otherwise known as a garnishee) against your debtor. Under New York law, if your debtor's disposable earnings are $127.50 or less, you can not file this income execution. If your debtor's disposable earnings are more than $127.50 and less than $170.00, you can file an income execution for the lesser of the excess over $127.50 or ten percent of his or her gross income. If your debtor's disposable earnings are $170.00 or more, you can file an income execution for the lesser of twenty-five percent of disposable earnings, or ten percent of gross income.

The rules governing the issuance of a property execution also apply to the issuance of an income execution. (See prior section; PROPERTY EXECUTION.) An income execution which is delivered to the sheriff must contain the following statement:

THIS INCOME EXECUTION DIRECTS THE WITHHOLDING OF UP TO TEN PER-CENT OF THE JUDGMENTS DEBTOR'S GROSS INCOME. IN CERTAIN CASES, HOWEVER, STATE OR FEDERAL LAW DOES NOT PERMIT THE WITHHOLDING

OF THAT MUCH OF THE JUDGMENT DEBTOR'S GROSS INCOME. THE JUDGMENT DEBTOR IS REFERRED TO NEW YORK CIVIL PRACTICE LAW AND RULES §5231 AND 15 UNITED STATES CODE §1671 ET SEQ.

I. LIMITATIONS ON THE AMOUNT THAT CAN BE WITHHELD.

A. AN INCOME EXECUTION FOR INSTALLMENTS FROM A JUDGMENT DEBTOR'S GROSS INCOME CANNOT EXCEED TEN PERCENT (10%) OF THE JUDGMENT DEBTOR'S GROSS INCOME.

B. IF A JUDGMENT DEBTOR'S WEEKLY DISPOSABLE EARNINGS ARE LESS THAN THIRTY (30) TIMES THE CURRENT FEDERAL MINIMUM WAGE ($4.25, PER HOUR), OR (127.50), NO DEDUCTION CAN BE MADE FROM THE JUDGMENT DEBTOR'S EARNINGS UNDER THIS INCOME EXECUTION.

C. A JUDGMENT DEBTOR'S WEEKLY DISPOSABLE EARNINGS CANNOT BE REDUCED BELOW THE AMOUNT ARRIVED AT BY MULTIPLYING THIRTY (30) TIMES THE CURRENT FEDERAL MINIMUM WAGE ($4.25, PER HOUR), OR ($127.50), UNDER THIS INCOME EXECUTION.

D. IF DEDUCTIONS ARE BEING MADE FROM A JUDGMENT DEBTOR'S EARNINGS UNDER ANY ORDER FOR ALIMONY, SUPPORT OR MAINTENANCE FOR FAMILY MEMBERS OR FORMER SPOUSES, AND THOSE DEDUCTIONS EQUAL OR EXCEED TWENTY-FIVE PERCENT (25%) OF THE JUDGMENT DEBTOR'S DISPOSABLE EARNINGS, NO DEDUCTION CAN BE MADE FROM THE JUDGMENT DEBTOR'S EARNINGS UNDER THIS INCOME EXECUTION.

E. IF DEDUCTIONS ARE BEING MADE FROM A JUDGMENT DEBTOR'S EARNINGS UNDER ANY ORDERS FOR ALIMONY SUPPORT OR MAINTENANCE FOR FAMILY MEMBERS OR FORMER SPOUSES, AND THOSE DEDUCTIONS ARE LESS THAN TWENTY-FIVE PERCENT (25%) OF THE JUDGMENT DEBTOR'S DISPOSABLE EARNINGS, DEDUCTIONS MAY BE MADE FROM THE JUDGMENT DEBTOR'S EARNINGS UNDER THIS INCOME EXECUTION. HOWEVER, THE AMOUNT ARRIVED AT BY ADDING THE DEDUCTIONS FROM EARNINGS MADE UNDER THIS EXECUTION TO THE DEDUCTIONS MADE FROM EARNINGS UNDER ANY ORDERS FOR ALIMONY, SUPPORT OR MAINTENANCE FOR FAMILY MEMBERS OR FORMER SPOUSES CANNOT EXCEED TWENTY-FIVE PERCENT (25%) OF THE JUDGMENT DEBTOR'S DISPOSABLE EARNINGS.

NOTE: NOTHING IN THIS NOTICE LIMITS THE PROPORTION OR AMOUNT WHICH MAY BE DEDUCTED UNDER ANY ORDER FOR ALIMONY, SUPPORT OR MAINTENANCE FOR FAMILY MEMBERS OR FORMER SPOUSES.

II. EXPLANATION OF LIMITATIONS

DEFINITIONS:

DISPOSABLE EARNINGS

DISPOSABLE EARNINGS ARE THAT PART OF AN INDIVIDUAL'S EARNINGS LEFT AFTER DEDUCTING THOSE AMOUNTS THAT ARE REQUIRED BY LAW TO BE WITHHELD (FOR EXAMPLE, TAXES, SOCIAL SECURITY, AND UNEMPLOYMENT INSURANCE, BUT NO DEDUCTIONS FOR UNION DUES, INSURANCE PLANS. ETC.).

GROSS INCOME

GROSS INCOME IS SALARY, WAGES OR OTHER INCOME, INCLUDING ANY AND ALL OVERTIME EARNINGS, COMMISSIONS, AND INCOME FROM TRUSTS, BEFORE ANY DEDUCTIONS ARE MADE FROM SUCH INCOME.

ILLUSTRATIONS REGARDING EARNINGS:

IF DISPOSABLE EARNINGS IS:	AMOUNT TO PAY OR DEDUCT UNDER THIS INCOME EXECUTION IS:
(a) 30 TIMES FEDERAL MINIMUM WAGE ($127.50) OR LESS	
(b) MORE THAN 30 TIMES FEDERAL MINIMUM WAGE ($127.50) AND LESS THAN 40 TIMES FEDERAL MINIMUM WAGE ($170.00)	THE LESSER OF: THE EXCESS OVER 30 TIMES THE FEDERAL MINIMUM WAGE ($127.50) IN DISPOSABLE EARNINGS, OR 10% OF GROSS EARNINGS
(c) 40 TIMES THE FEDERAL MINIMUM WAGE ($170.00) OR MORE	THE LESSER OF: 25% OF DISPOSABLE EARNINGS OR 10% OF GROSS EARNINGS.

III. NOTICE: YOU MAY BE ABLE TO CHALLENGE THIS INCOME EXECUTION THROUGH THE PROCEDURES PROVIDED IN CPLR §5231(I) AND CPLR §5240

IF YOU THINK THAT THE AMOUNT OF YOUR INCOME BEING DEDUCTED UNDER THIS INCOME EXECUTION EXCEEDS THE AMOUNT PERMITTED BY STATE OR FEDERAL LAW, YOU SHOULD ACT PROMPTLY BECAUSE THE MONEY WILL BE APPLIED TO THE JUDGMENT IF YOU CLAIM THAT THE AMOUNT OF YOUR INCOME BEING DEDUCTED UNDER THIS INCOME EXECUTION EXCEEDS THE AMOUNT PERMITTED BY STATE OR FEDERAL LAW, YOU SHOULD CONTACT YOUR EMPLOYER OR OTHER PERSON PAYING YOUR INCOME. FURTHER, YOU MAY CONSULT AN ATTORNEY, INCLUDING LEGAL AID IF YOU QUALIFY. NEW YORK STATE LAW PROVIDES TWO PROCEDURES THROUGH WHICH AN INCOME EXECUTION CAN BE CHALLENGED:

CPLR §5231(I) MODIFICATION. AT ANY TIME, THE JUDGMENT DEBTOR MAY MAKE A MOTION TO A COURT FOR AN ORDER MODIFYING AN INCOME EXECUTION.

CPLR §5240 MODIFICATION OR PROTECTIVE ORDER: SUPERVISION OR ENFORCEMENT. AT ANY TIME, THE JUDGMENT DEBTOR MAY MAKE A MOTION TO A COURT FOR AN ORDER DENYING, LIMITING, CONDITIONING, REGULATING, EXTENDING OR MODIFYING THE USE OF ANY POST-JUDGMENT ENFORCEMENT PROCEDURE, INCLUDING THE USE OF INCOME EXECUTIONS.

BANKRUPTCY

If the defendant files bankruptcy, all legal actions must immediately stop. You can be held in contempt of federal court if you take any action to further your case or acquire the defendant's property. If the defendant files liquidation bankruptcy then your claim is wiped out and you are forever barred from collecting on it. If the defendant files reorganization bankruptcy, you may be paid at a later time in full or in part. If a bankruptcy is withdrawn before the debtor is discharged, you may proceed with your claim.

IF YOUR JUDGMENT INVOLVES THE DEFENDANT'S BUSINESS

If your judgment was based on dealing with the defendant's business, there are some other rules that you should consider in respect to enforcement of your judgment. For example, you (the judgment creditor) may be entitled to bring a second lawsuit against your judgment debtor for triple the amount of your judgment which your debtor refuses to pay, plus all reasonable attorney fees, plus the costs and disbursement of this second action if the following conditions are met: a) there is a recorded judgment in your favor in a small claims court; b) your judgment must have resulted from a transactions in the course of your judgment debtor's trade or business or out of a repeated course of dealing or conduct of your debtor; c) there are at least two other unsatisfied recorded judgments of a small claims court arising out of your debtor's trade or business or repeated course of dealing or conduct. Since unsatisfied small claims court judgments are required to be indexed alphabetically and chronologically under the name of a defendant, you should be able to ascertain this condition quite quickly; and, d) you must have given your judgment debtor notice of your judgment by certified mail, return receipt requested, and your debtor has failed to satisfy your judgment within thirty days after receipt of this notice. Your notice must contain a statement that your judgment exists, that at least two other unsatisfied recorded judgments exist, and that failure to pay your judgment may be the basis for an action for treble the amount of your unsatisfied judgment.

Even if all of the above conditions exist and you bring a second suit, your judgment debtor will have a defense against such action if he or she did not have resources to satisfy your judgment within thirty days after receipt of notice.

Another rule should be aware of relates to judgments involving activities for which a license is required. Under New York law, whenever a judgment which relates to activities for which a license is required has been rendered against a business which is licensed by a state or local licensing authority and which remains unpaid for thirty-five days after receipt by the judgment debtor of notice of its entry and the judgment has not been stayed or appealed, the state or local licensing authority must consider such failure to pay, if deliberate, or part of a pattern of similar conduct indicating recklessness, as a basis for the revocation, suspension, conditioning or refusal to grant or renew such a license. You may find this law beneficial in persuading your debtor to satisfy your judgment since any license will surely have great value to your debtor.

You should also be aware that New York Law provides the if a defendant appears to be engaged in repeated fraudulent or illegal acts or other wise demonstrates persistent fraud or illegality in the carrying on, conducting or transaction of business, that the court must either advise the attorney general or advise you to do the same, and that the court must also advise the appropriate state of local licensing or certifying authority or advise you to do the same.

WHERE JUDGMENT IS RENDERED IN OTHER THAN THE TRUE NAME OF THE DEFENDANT

Surprising enough, you are actually rewarded when your judgment is rendered in a name other than the true name of the defendant and remains unsatisfied. The true name means the legal name of a natural person and the name under which a partnership, firm, or corporation is licensed, registered, incorporated or otherwise authorized to do business.

Under New York law, if a judgment was rendered in a name other than the true name of such a judgment debtor and has remained unpaid for thirty-five days after receipt by the judgment debtor of notice of its entry, you are entitled to commence an action in small claims court or any other court of competent jurisdiction against such debtor, notwithstanding the jurisdictional limit of the court, for the sum of your original judgment, plus reasonable attorney's fees, plus $100. This should be an incentive for judgment debtors to disclose their true name!

APPEALING

VACATING A DEFAULT

A defendant who fails to appear at the hearing on the day and time fixed will be held in default, except that no default can be ordered if the defendant or his attorney appears within one hour after the time fixed for the hearing.

Clearly, having a default judgment rendered against you is not a good position to be in. You should make every effort to attend your hearing; otherwise, you will more likely than not have lost your case without ever having an opportunity to put forward your case. If you are in a position where you find that you can not attend your hearing, you should make every effort to notify the court *prior* to the time that a default judgment is rendered against you.

If a default judgment has been rendered against you by a small claims court, the small claims court has the power to relieve you from this judgment upon the ground of excusable default. Generally, excusable default means that your default must be excusable, and you must show that you have either a meritorious claim or defense to the action. Examples of excusable default might be where you did not receive any actual notice of the lawsuit, or you believed your attorney was handling your case. A form that you can use for your motion to vacate a default judgment is contained in appendix B.

FILING AN APPEAL

After losing a hard-fought case, a person's first reaction is to promise an appeal. However, one must realize that appeals of small claims judgments are difficult to win.

When a trial court hears a case, it decides questions of fact and questions of law. Usually the questions of fact are most important: Were the repairs done correctly? Was the bill paid in cash? Was a notice mailed to the tenant? Questions of law concern the legal rights of the parties under those facts.

Questions of fact are never appealable. An appeals court can only review the *legal* decision of the judge, which is not often wrong. If the judge didn't believe you did a good repair job or didn't believe one of your witnesses, you don't get a second chance to convince an appeals court or to bring more witnesses. The appeals court will review the legal decision of the judge and accept all of his fact findings. Only if the judge made an obvious legal mistake will the judgment be overturned.

In addition to the restriction that an appeals court can only review questions of law, an appeals court can only review those questions of law which are substantive in nature. Legal principals which are procedural in nature such as how the evidence was presented at your hearing or not reviewable in a small claims case.

Our legal system is not perfect. Sometimes liars win and there is no way to reverse the decision. The best you can do is be prepared for your trial with the evidence at your disposal.

If you feel the judge made an error of law in deciding your case, you can file a Notice of Appeal within thirty days of the judgment. The clerk of the small claims court should be of assistance in telling you how to file your notice. If the clerk does not provide you with a form that you can use, you can use the NOTICE OF APPEAL form in appendix B.

In most cases you will appeal your case to the county court unless and appellate term of the Supreme Court has been established to hear such appeals. Appeals from the New York City Civil Court are taken to the appellate division of the Supreme Court unless an appellate term of the Supreme Court has been established to hear such appeals. Again, the clerk of the small claims court should be of assistance in telling you the correct court to appeal your case. After you have completed filling out your notice of appeal, you must mail a copy to your opposing party and file another copy with the clerk of the small claim court.

Another obstacle to an appeal is the requirement that you furnish the appeals court with a record of your hearing before the small claims court judge. The procedure can be costly and time consuming for you. For example, in the case where no stenographic record of your hearing was made, you must mail to your opponent a statement of the proceedings from your own recollection. The opponent may then mail to you any objections or proposed amendments to this statement and then all of this material must be submitted for settlement to the judge who heard your case. If a stenographic record of your proceedings were made, you will be required to purchase this record from the court reporter and go through a similar procedure of sending a copy to your opponent and waiting for any objections made to the transcript. The best advice to properly file your appeal is to obtain from your appeals court their own rules on how you prefect your appeal. You can also look at the rules on appeals contained in Civil Practice Law and Rules Article 55.

The mailing of a notice of appeal will automatically stay (prevent) all proceedings to enforce a judgment for the payment of money pending the appeal where you (the appellant) furnish an undertaking with the court in the amount of the judgment. If you do not furnish this undertaking, your opponent may still be able to enforce the judgment while your appeal is progress.

DEADLINES

Appeals must be filed within thirty days of the judgment. Since the procedure can be complicated, it is usually advantageous to seek the advice of an attorney.

SMALL CLAIMS CHECKLIST

FOR DEFENDANT

1. Prior to Trial (Hearing):
   Have you tried to work it out with the other side?
   Should you hire a lawyer?
   Do you have a defense which would bar the claim?
   Should you countersue or implead another defendant?
   Gather all the evidence.
   Subpoena witnesses and evidence if necessary.

2. Attend the trial:
   Be prepared to explain your side clearly and quickly
   Be on time/Dress appropriately/Be polite
   Be prepared to settle if the plaintiff makes a good offer

3. After the trial:

If you won a countersuit:
   See if plaintiff plans to pay
   Docket your judgment
   If Plaintiff refuses to pay
      the following:
      a. Serving an information subpoena.
      b. Issuing a property execution.
      c. Issuing an income execution.

If you lost:
   Should you stipulate to avoid a judgment?
   Was it a default which can be vacated?
   Should you request a rehearing?
   Is there an issue to appeal?
   Should you pay?

FOR PLAINTIFF

1. **Decide if you should sue:**
   Did you try to work it out with the other side?
   Is there a legal theory which would make the defendant liable?
   Do you have enough evidence to win the case?
   Does the defendant have any defenses?
   Does the defendant have any money or property you could seize?

2. **Prepare your case:**
   Gather evidence
   Talk to witnesses
   Prepare your statement of claim
   File your case

3. **Before the trial:**
   Gather all the evidence
   Subpoena witnesses and evidence if necessary

4. **Attend the trial:**
   Be prepared
   Be on time/Dress appropriately/Be polite
   Be prepared to settle if the defendant makes a good offer

5. **After the trial:**

If you won a countersuit:
   See if defendant plans to pay
   Docket your judgment
   If the defendant refuses to pay
   consider the following:
   a. Serving an information subpoena
   b. Issuing a property execution.
   c. Issuing an income execution.

If you lost:
   Should you stipulate to avoid a judgment?
   Was it a default which can be vacated?
   Should you request a rehearing?
   Is there an issue to appeal?
   Should you pay?

APPENDIX A
NEW YORK
SMALL CLAIMS RULES

Listed below are the laws of New York which will be most relevant to your case. If you wish to obtain clarification or proof for something written in this book, your best bet is to consult these laws since they make up the greatest percentage of laws that are applicable to how a small claims or commercial claims case proceeds. We have included the City Court rules in this appendix. You should be able to find the other laws in the legal section of your library. However, some libraries may not have all of these laws, in which case you will need to go to a law library. You can find law libraries at law schools, and near your local Courthouse.

If you are suing in a **city court**, your case will be governed by the **Uniform City Court Act §§1801-1814 (§§1801A-1814A for commercial claims)** as well as by the **Uniform Civil Rules for the City Courts outside the City of New York §210.41 (§210.41a for commercial claims)**.

If you are suing in the **New York City Civil Court** your case will be governed by the **New York City Civil Court Act §§1801-1814 (1801A-1814A for commercial claims)** as well as by the **Uniform Civil Rules for the New York City Civil Court §208.41 (§208.41a for commercial claims)**.

If you are suing in a **Town or Village court**, your case will be governed by the **Uniform Justice Court Act §§1801-1814** as well as by the **Uniform Civil Rules for the Justice Courts §214.10.**

If you are suing in a **District Court**, your case will be governed by the **Uniform District Court Act §§1801-1814 (§§1801A-1814A for commercial claims)** as well as by the **Uniform Rules for the District Courts §212.41 (§212.41a for commercial claims).**

Article 18
Small Claims

§1801. Small claims defined

The term "small claim" or "small claims" as used in this act shall mean and include any cause of action for money only not in excess of *three* thousand dollars exclusive of interest and costs, provided that the defendant either resides, or has an office for the transaction of business or a regular employment, within the county. In a city court having a basic monetary jurisdiction in civil matters of less than one thousand dollars, the small claims jurisdiction of such court shall be equal to its basic monetary jurisdiction.

§1802. Parts for the determination of small claims established

The chief administrator shall assign the times and places for holding, and the judges who shall hold, one or more parts or the court for the hearing of small claims as herein defined, and the rules may regulate the practice and procedure controlling the determination of such claims and prescribe and furnish the forms for instituting the same. There shall be at least one evening session of each part every month for the hearing of small claims, provided however, that the chief administrator may provide for exemption from this requirement where there exists no demonstrated need for evening sessions. Such practice, procedure and forms shall differ from the practice, procedure and forms used in the court for other than small claims, notwithstanding any provision of law to the contrary. They shall constitute a simple, informal and inexpensive procedure for the prompt determination of commercial claims in accordance with the rules and principles of substantive law. The procedure established pursuant to this article shall not be exclusive of but shall be alternative to the procedure now or hereafter established with respect to actions commenced in the court by the service of a summons. No rule to be enacted pursuant to this article shall dispense with or interfere with the taking of stenographic minutes of any hearing of any small claim hereunder, except that in cities with a population of fifty thousand or less hearings may be recorded mechanically.

§1803. Commencement of action upon commercial claims

(a) Small claims shall be commenced upon the payment by the claimant of a filing fee of three dollars and the cost of mailings as herein provided, without the service of a summons and, except by special order of the court, without the service of any pleading other than a statement of his cause of action by the claimant or someone in his behalf to the clerk, who shall reduce the same to a concise, written form and record it in a docket kept especially for such purpose. Such procedure shall provide for the sending of notice of such claim by ordinary first class mail and certified mail with return receipt requested to the party complained against at his residence, if he resides within the county, and his residence is known to the claimant, or at his office or place of regular employment within the county if he does not reside therein or his residence within the county is not known to the claimant. If, after the expiration of twenty-one days, such ordinary first class mailing has not been returned as undeliverable, the party complained against shall be presumed to have received notice of such claim.

Such procedure shall further provide for an early hearing upon and determination of such claim. No filing fee, however, shall be demanded or received on small claims of employees who shall comply with § 1912 of this act which is hereby made applicable, except that necessary mailing costs shall be paid.

(b) The clerk shall furnish every claimant, upon commencement of the action, and every party complained against, with the notice of claim, and with information written in clear and coherent language which shall be prescribed and furnished by the office of court administration, concerning the small claims court. Such information shall include, but not be limited to, an explanation of the following terms and procedures; adjournments, counterclaims, jury trial requests, subpoenas, arbitration and collection methods and fees, *the responsibility of the judgment creditor to collect data on the judgment debtor's assets, the ability of the court prior to entering judgment to order examination of or disclosure by, the defendant and restrain him,* the utilization of section eighteen hundred twelve of this article concerning treble damage awards and information subpoenas including, but not limited to, specific questions to be used on information subpoenas, and the claimant's right to notify the appropriate state or local licensing or certifying authority of an unsatisfied judgment if it arises out of the carrying on, conducting or transaction of a licensed or certified business or if such business appears to be engaged in fraudulent or illegal acts or otherwise demonstrates fraud or illegality in the carrying on, conducting or transaction of its business *and a list of at least the most prominent state or local licensing or certifying authorities and a description of the business categories such licensing or certifying authorities oversee.* The information shall be available in English. Large signs in English shall be posted in conspicuous locations in each small claims court clerk's office, advising the public of its availability.

§1804. Informal and simplified procedure on commercial claims

The court shall conduct hearings upon small claims in such manner as to do substantial justice between the parties according to the rules of substantive law and shall not be bound by statutory provisions or rules of practice, procedure, pleading or evidence except statutory provisions relating to privileged communications and personal transactions or communications with a decedent or mentally ill person. An itemized bill or invoice, receipted or marked paid, or two itemized estimates for services or repairs, are admissible in evidence and are prima facie evidence of the reasonable value and necessity of such services and repairs. Disclosure shall be unavailable in small claims procedure except upon order of the court on showing of proper circumstances. *In every small claims action, where the claim arises out of the conduct of the defendant's business at the hearing on the matter, the judge or arbitrator shall determine the appropriate state or local licensing or certifying authorities and any business or professional association of which the defendant is a member.* The provisions of this act and the rules of this court, together with the statutes and rules governing supreme court practice, shall apply to claims brought under this article so far as the same can be made applicable and are not in conflict with the provisions of this article; in case of conflict, the provisions of this article shall control.

§1805. Remedies available; transfer of commercial claims

(a) Upon determination of a small claim, the court shall direct judgment in accordance with its findings, and, when necessary to do substantial justice between the parties, may condition the entry of judgment upon such terms as the court shall deem proper. *Pursuant to section fifty-two hundred twenty-nine of the civil practice law and rules prior to entering a judgment, the court may order the examination of or disclosure by, the defendant and restrain him to the same extent as if a restraining notice had been served upon him after judgment was entered.*

(b) The court shall have power to transfer any small claim or claims to any other part of the court upon such terms as the rules may provide, and proceed to hear the same according to the usual practice and procedure applicable to other parts of the court.

(c) No counterclaim shall be permitted in a small claims action, unless the court would have had monetary jurisdiction over the counterclaim if it had been filed as a small claim. Any other claim sought to be maintained against the claimant may be filed in any court of competent jurisdiction.

(d) If the defendant appears to be engaged in repeated fraudulent or illegal acts or otherwise demonstrates persistent fraud or illegality in the carrying on, conducting, or transaction of business, the court shall either advise the attorney general in relation to his authority under subdivision twelve of section sixty-three of the executive law, or shall advise the claimant to do same, but shall retain jurisdiction over the small claim.

(e) If the defendant appears to be engaged in fraudulent or illegal acts or otherwise demonstrates fraud or illegality in the carrying on, conducting or transaction of a licensed or certified business, the court shall either advise the appropriate state or local licensing or certifying authority or shall advise the claimant to do same, but shall retain jurisdiction over the small claim.

§1806. Trial by jury; how obtained; discretionary costs

A person commencing an action upon a small claim under this article shall be deemed to have waived a trial by jury, but if said action shall be removed to a regular part of the court, the plaintiff shall have the same right to demand a trial by jury as if such action had originally been begun in such part. Any party to such action, other than the plaintiff, prior to the day upon which he is notified to appear or answer, may file with the court a demand for a trial by jury and his affidavit that there are issues of fact in the action requiring such a trial, specifying the same and stating that such trial is desired and intended in good faith. Such demand and affidavit shall be accompanied with the jury fee required by law and an undertaking in the sum of fifty dollars in such form as may be approved by the rules, payable to the other party or parties, conditioned upon the payment of any costs which may be entered against him in the said action or any appeal within thirty days after the entry thereof; or, in lieu of said undertaking, the sum of fifty dollars may be deposited with the clerk of the court and thereupon the clerk shall forthwith transmit such original papers or duly attested copies thereof as may be provided by the rules to the part of the court to which the action shall have been transferred and assigned and such part may require pleadings in such action as though it had been begun by the service of a summons. Such action may be considered a preferred cause of action. In any small claim which may have been transferred to another part of the court, the court may award costs up to twenty-five dollars to the claimant if the plaintiff prevails.

§1807. Proceedings on default and review of judgments

A person commencing an action upon a small claim under this article shall be deemed to have waived all right to appeal, except that either party may appeal on the sole grounds that substantial justice has not been done between the parties according to the rules and principles of substantive law.

§1808. Judgment obtained to be res judicata in certain cases

A judgment obtained under this article may be pleaded as res judicata only as to the amount involved in the particular action and shall not otherwise be deemed an adjudication of any fact at issue or found therein in any other action or court.

§1809. Procedures relating to corporations, associations, insurers and assignees

No corporation, except a municipal corporation or public benefit corporation, school district or school district public library wholly or partially within the municipal corporate limit, no partnership, or association and no assignee of any small claim shall institute an action or proceeding under this article, nor shall this article apply to any claim or cause of action brought by an insurer in its own name or in the name of its insured whether before or after payment to the insured on the policy.

A corporation may appear in the defense of any small claim action brought pursuant to this article by an attorney as well as by any authorized officer, director or employee of the corporation provided that the appearance by a non-lawyer on behalf of a corporation shall be deemed to constitute the requisite authority to bind the corporation in a settlement or trial. The court or arbitrator may make reasonable inquiry to determine the authority of any person who appears for the corporation in defense of a small claims court case.

§1810. Limitation on right to resort to commercial claims procedures

If the clerk shall find that the procedures of the small claims part are sought to be utilized by a claimant for purposes of oppression or harassment, as where a claimant has previously resorted to such procedures on the same claim and has been unsuccessful after the hearing thereon, the clerk may in his discretion compel the claimant to make application to the court for leave to prosecute the claim in the small claim part. The court upon such application may inquire into the circumstances and, if it shall find that the claim has already been adjudicated, or that the claim is sought to be brought on solely for purposes of oppression or harassment and not under color of right, it may make an order denying the claimant the use of the small claims part to prosecute the claim.

§1811. Notice of small claims judgments and indexing of unpaid claims

(a) Notice of judgment sent to judgment debtor shall specify that a failure to satisfy a judgment may subject the debtor to any one or combination of the following actions:

1. garnishment of wage;
2. garnishment of bank account;
3. a lien on personal property;
4. seizure and sale of real property;
5. seizure and sale of personal property, including automobiles;
6. suspension of motor vehicle license and registration, if claim is based on defendant's ownership or operation of a motor vehicle;
7. revocation, suspension, or denial of renewal of any applicable business license or permit;
8. investigation and prosecution by the attorney general for fraudulent or illegal business practices; and
9. a penalty equal to three times the amount of the unsatisfied judgment plus attorney's fees, if there are other unpaid claims.

(b) Notice of judgment sent to judgment creditor shall contain but not be limited to the following information:

1. the claimant's right to payment within thirty days following the debtor's receipt of the judgment notice.
2. the procedures for use of section eighteen hundred twelve of this article concerning the identification of assets of the judgment debtor *including the use of information subpoenas, access to consumer credit reports and the role of sheriffs and marshals,* and actions to collect three times the judgment award and attorney's fees if there are two other unsatisfied claims against the debtor;
3. the claimant's right to initiate actions to recover the unpaid judgment through the sale of the debtor's real property, or personal property;
4. the claimant's right to initiate actions to recover the unpaid judgment through suspension of debtor's motor vehicle license and registration, if claim is based on defendant's ownership or operation of a motor vehicle;
5. the claimant's right to notify the appropriate state or local licensing or certifying authority of an unsatisfied judgment as a basis for possible revocation, suspension, or denial of renewal of business license; and
6. a statement that upon satisfying the judgment, the judgment debtor shall present appropriate proof thereof to the court; and
7. the claimant's right to notify the attorney general if the debtor is a business and appears to be engaged in fraudulent or illegal business practices.

(c) All wholly or partially unsatisfied small claims court judgments shall be indexed alphabetically and chronologically under the name of the defendant. *Upon satisfying the judgment, the defendant shall present appropriate proof to the court and the court shall indicate such in the records.*

§1812. Enforcement of small claims judgments

(a) The special procedures set forth in subdivision (b) hereof shall be available only where:

1. there is a recorded judgment of a small claims court; and
2. (i) the aforesaid judgment resulted from a transaction in the course of the trade or business of the judgment debtor, or arose out of a repeated course of dealing or conduct of the judgment debtor, and (ii) there are at least two other unsatisfied recorded judgments of a small claims court arising out of such trade or business or repeated course of dealing or conduct, against that judgment debtor; and
3. the judgment debtor failed to satisfy such judgment within a period of thirty days after receipt of notice of such judgment. Such notice shall be given in the same manner as provided for the service of a summons or by certified mail, return receipt requested, and shall contain a statement that such judgment exists, that at least two other unsatisfied recorded judgments exist, and that failure to pay such judgment may be the basis for an action, for treble the amount of such unsatisfied judgment, pursuant to this section.

(b) Where each of the elements of subdivision (a) of this section are present the judgment creditor shall be entitled to commence an action against said judgment debtor for treble the amount of such unsatisfied judgment, together with reasonable counsel fees, and the cost and disbursements of such action, provided, however, that in any such action it shall be a defense that the judgment debtor did not have resources to satisfy such judgment within a period of thirty days after receipt of notice of such judgment. The failure to pay a judgment obtained in an action pursuant to this section shall not be the basis for another such action pursuant to this section.

(c) Where the judgment is obtained in an action pursuant to subdivision (b), and arises from a business of the defendant, the court shall, in addition to its responsibilities under this article, advise the attorney general in relation to his authority under subdivision twelve of section sixty-three of the executive law, and if such judgment arises from a certified or licensed business of the defendant, advise the state or local licensing or certifying authority.

(d) Where a judgment has been entered in a small claims court and remains unsatisfied, the small claims clerk shall, upon request, issue information subpoenas, at nominal cost, for the judgment creditor and provide the creditor with assistance on their preparation and use. *The court shall have the same power as the supreme court to punish a contempt of court committed with respect to an information subpoena.*

§1813. Duty to pay judgments

(a) Any person, partnership, firm or corporation which is sued a small claims court for any cause of action arising out of business activities, shall pay any judgment rendered against it in true name or in any name in which it conducts business. "True name" includes the legal name of a natural person and the name under which a partnership, firm or corporation is licensed, registered, incorporated or otherwise authorized to do business. "Conducting business" as used in this section shall include, but not limited to, maintaining signs at business premises or on business vehicles; advertising; entering into contracts; and printing or using sales slips, checks, invoices or receipts. Whenever a judgment has been rendered against a person, partnership, firm or corporation other than its true name and the judgment has remained unpaid

thirty-five days after receipt by the judgment debtor of notice of its entry, the aggrieved judgment creditor shall be entitled to commence an action in small claims court against such judgment debtor, notwithstanding the jurisdictional limit of the court, for the sum of the original judgment, costs, reasonable attorney's fees, and one hundred dollars.

(b) Whenever a judgment which relates to activities for which a license is required has been rendered against a business which is licensed by a state or local licensing authority and which remains unpaid for thirty-five days after receipt by the judgment debtor of notice of its entry and the judgment has not been stayed or appealed, the state or local licensing authority shall consider such failure to pay, if deliberate or part of a pattern of similar conduct indicating recklessness, as a basis for the revocation, suspension, conditioning or refusal to grant or renew such license. Nothing herein shall be construed to preempt an authority's existing policy if it is more restrictive.

(c) The clerk shall attach to the notice of suit required under this article a notice of the duty imposed by this section.

§1814. Designation of defendant; amendment procedure

(a) A party who is ignorant, in whole or in part, of the true name of a person, partnership, firm or corporation which may properly be made a party defendant, may proceed against such defendant in any name used by the person, partnership, firm or corporation in conducting business, as defined in subdivision (a) of section eighteen hundred thirteen of this article.

(b) If the true name of the defendant becomes known at any time prior to the hearing on the merits, such information shall be brought to the attention of the clerk, who shall immediately amend all prior proceedings and papers. The clerk shall send an amended notice to the defendant, without payment of additional fees by the plaintiff, and all subsequent proceedings and papers shall be amended accordingly.

(c) In every action in the small claims part, at the hearing on the merits, the judge or arbitrator shall determine the defendant's true name. The clerk shall amend all prior proceedings and papers to conform to such determination, and all subsequent proceedings and papers shall be amended accordingly.

(d) A party against whom a judgment has been entered pursuant to this article, in any proceeding under section five thousand fifteen of the civil practice law and rules for relief from such judgment, shall, disclose its true name; any and all names in which it is conducting business; and any and all names in which it was conducting business at the time of the transaction or occurrence on which such judgment is based. All subsequent proceedings and papers shall be amended to conform to such disclosure.

§1815. Appearance by non-attorney representatives

The court may permit, upon the request of a party, that a non-attorney representative, who is related by consanguinity or affinity to such party, be allowed to appear on behalf of such party when the court finds that due to the age, mental or physical capacity or other disability of such party that it is in the interests of justice to permit such representation. No person acting as a non-attorney representative shall be permitted to charge a fee or be allowed to accept any form of remuneration for such services.

ARTICLE 18-A — COMMERCIAL CLAIMS

§1801-A. Commercial claims defined

(a) The term "commercial claim" or "commercial claims" as used in this act shall mean and include any cause of action for money only not in excess of the maximum amount permitted for a small claim in the small claims part of the court, exclusive of interest and costs, provided that subject to the limitations contained in section eighteen hundred nine-A of this article, the claimant is a corporation, partnership or association, which has its principal office in the state of New York and provided that the defendant either resides, or has an office for the transaction of business or a regular employment, within the county in which the court is located. In a city court having a basic monetary jurisdiction in civil matters of less than one thousand dollars, the commercial claims jurisdiction of such court shall be equal to its basic monetary jurisdiction.

(b) Consumer transaction defined. The term "consumer transaction" means a transaction between a claimant and a natural person, wherein the money property or service which is the subject of the transaction is primarily for personal, family or household purposes.

§1802-A. Parts for the determination of commercial claims established

The chief administrator shall assign the times and places for holding, and the judges who shall hold, one or more parts of the court for the hearing of commercial claims as herein defined, and the rules may regulate the practice and procedure controlling the determination of such claims and prescribe and furnish the forms for instituting the same. There shall be at least one evening session of each part every month for the hearing of commercial claims, provided however, that the chief administrator may provide for exemption from this requirement where there exists no demonstrated need for evening sessions. The chief administrator shall not combine commercial claims part actions with small claims part actions for purposes of convenience unless a preference is given to small claims and to commercial claims arising out of consumer transactions. Such practice, procedure and forms shall differ from the practice, procedure and forms used in the court for other than small claims and commer-

cial claims, notwithstanding any provision of law to the contrary. They shall constitute a simple, informal and inexpensive procedure for the prompt determination of commercial claims in accordance with the rules and principles of substantive law. The procedure established pursuant to this article shall not be exclusive of but shall be alternative to the procedure now or hereafter established with respect to actions commenced in the court by the service of a summons. No rule to be enacted pursuant to this article shall dispense with or interfere with the taking of stenographic minutes of any hearing of any business claim hereunder, except that in cities with a population of fifty thousand or less hearings may be recorded mechanically.

§1803-A. Commencement of action upon commercial claims

(a) Commercial claims other than claims arising out of consumer transactions shall be commenced upon the payment by the claimant of a filing fee of twenty dollars and the cost of mailings as herein provided, without the service of a summons and, except by special order of the court, without the service of any pleading other than a required certification verified as to its truthfulness by the claimant on a form prescribed by the state office of court administration and filed with the clerk, that no more than five such actions or proceedings (including the instant action or proceeding) have been instituted during that calendar month, and a statement of its cause of action by the claimant or someone in its behalf to the clerk, who shall reduce the same to a concise, written form and record it in a docket kept especially for such purpose. Such procedure shall provide that the commercial claims part of the court shall have no jurisdiction over, and shall dismiss, any case with respect to which the required certification is not made upon the attempted institution of the action of proceeding. Such procedure shall provide for the sending of notice of such claim by ordinary first class mail and certified mail with return receipt requested to the party complained against at his residence, if he resides within the county in which the court is located, and his residence is known to the claimant, or at his office or place of regular employment within such county if he does not reside therein or his residence within the county is not known to the claimant. If, after the expiration of twenty-one days, such ordinary first class mailing has not been returned as undeliverable, the party complained against shall be presumed to have received notice of such claim.

Such procedure shall further provide for an early hearing upon and determination of such claim. The hearing shall be scheduled in a manner which, to the extent possible, minimizes the time the party complained against must be absent from employment.

Either party may request that the hearing be scheduled during evening hours, provided that the hearing shall not be scheduled during evening hours if it would cause unreasonable hardship to either party. The court shall not unreasonably deny requests for evening hearings if such requests are made by the claimant upon commencement of the action or by the party complained against within fourteen days of receipt of the notice of claim.

(b) Commercial claims in actions arising out of consumer transactions shall be commenced upon the payment by the claimant of a filing fee of twenty dollars and the cost of mailings as herein provided, without the service of a summons and, except by special order of the court, without the service of any pleading other than a required statement of the cause of action by the claimant or someone on its behalf to the clerk, who shall reduce the same to a concise written form including the information required by subdivision (c) of this section, denominate it conspicuously as a consumer transaction, and record it in the docket marked as a consumer transaction, and by filing with the clerk a required certificate verified as to its truthfulness by the claimant on forms prescribed by the state office of court administration.

Such verified certificate shall certify (i) that the claimant has mailed by ordinary first class mail to the party complained against a demand letter, no less than ten days and no more than one hundred eighty days prior to the commencement of the claim, and (ii) that, based upon information and belief, the claimant has not instituted more than five actions or proceedings (including the instant action or proceeding) during the calendar month.

A form for the demand letter shall be prescribed and furnished by the state office of court administration and shall require the following information: The date of the consumer transaction; the amount that remains unpaid; a copy of the original debt instrument or other document underlying the debt and an accounting of all payments, and, if the claimant was not a party to the original transaction, the names and addresses of the parties to the original transaction; and a statement that the claimant intends to use this part of the court to obtain a judgment, that further notice of a hearing date will be sent, unless payment is received by a specified date, and that the party complained against will be entitled to appear at said hearing and present any defenses to the claim.;

In the event that the verified certificate is not properly completed by the claimant, the court shall not allow the action to proceed until the verified certificate is corrected. Notice of such claim shall be sent by the clerk by both ordinary first class mail and certified mail with return receipt requested to the party complained against at his residence, if he resides within the county in which the court is located, and his residence is known to the claimant, or at his office or place of regular employment within such county if he does not reside therein or his residence is not known to the claimant. If, after the expiration of thirty days, such ordinary first class mailing has not been returned as undeliverable, the party complained against shall be presumed to have received notice of such claim.

Such procedure shall further provide for an early hearing upon and determination of such claim. The hearing shall be scheduled in a manner which, to the extent possible, minimizes the time the party complained against must be absent from employment. Either party may request that the hearing be scheduled during evening hours, provided that the hearing shall not be scheduled during evening hours if it would cause unreasonable hardship to either party. The court shall not unreasonably deny requests for evening hearings if such requests are made by the claimant upon commencement of the action or by the party complained against within fourteen days of receipt of the notice of claim.

(c) The clerk shall furnish every claimant, upon commencement of the action, and every party complained against, with the notice of claim, and with information written in clear and coherent language which shall be prescribed and furnished by the state office of court administration, concerning the commercial claims part. Such information shall include, but not be limited to, the form for certification and filing by the claimant that no more than five such actions or proceedings have been instituted during that calendar month, and an explanation of the following terms and procedures; adjournments, counter claims, jury trial requests, evening hour requests, demand letters in cases concerning consumer transactions, default judgments, subpoenas, arbitration and collection methods, the responsibility of the judgment creditor to collect data on the judgment debtor's assets, the ability of the court prior to entering judgment to order examination of or disclosure by, the defendant and restrain him, and fees. The information shall be available in English and, if the chief administrator requires it, in Spanish shall be posted in conspicuous locations in each commercial claims part clerk's office, advising the public of its availability.

§1804-A. Informal and simplified procedure on commercial claims

The court shall conduct hearings upon commercial claims in such manner as to do substantial justice between the parties according to the rules of substantive law and shall not be bound by statutory provisions or rules of practice, procedure, pleading or evidence except statutory provisions relating to privileged communications and personal transactions or communications with a decedent or mentally ill person. An itemized bill or invoice, receipted or marked paid, or two itemized estimates for services or repairs, and admissible in evidence and are prima facie evidence of the reasonable value and necessity of such services and repairs. Disclosure shall be unavailable in commercial claims procedure except upon order of the court on showing of proper circumstances. The provisions of this act and the rules of this court, together with the statutes and rules governing supreme court practice, shall apply to claims brought under this article so far as the same can be made applicable and are not in conflict with the provisions of this article in case of conflict, the provisions of this article shall control.

§1805-A. Remedies available; transfer of commercial claims

(a) Upon determination of a commercial claim, the court shall direct judgment in accordance with

its findings, and, when necessary to do substantial justice between parties, may condition the entry of judgment upon such terms as the court shall deem proper. Pursuant to section fifty-two hundred twenty-nine of the civil practice law and rules prior to entering a judgment, the court may order the examination of or disclosure by, the defendant and restrain him to the same extent as if a restraining notice had been served upon him after judgment was entered.

(b) The court shall have power to transfer any commercial claim or claims to any other part of the court upon such terms as the rules may provide, and proceed to hear the same according to the usual practice and procedure applicable to other parts of the court.

(c) No counterclaim shall be permitted in a commercial claims action, unless the court would have had monetary jurisdiction over the counterclaim if it had been filed as a commercial claim. Any other claim sought to be maintained against the claimant may be filed in any court of competent jurisdiction.

(d) If the defendant appears to be engaged in repeated fraudulent or illegal acts or otherwise demonstrates persistent fraud or illegality in the carrying on, conducting, or transaction of business, the court shall either advise the attorney general in relation to his authority under subdivision twelve of section sixty-three of the executive law, or shall advise the claimant to do same, but shall retain jurisdiction over commercial claim.

(e) If the defendant appears to be engaged in fraudulent or illegal acts or otherwise demonstrates fraud or illegality in the carrying on, conducting or transaction of a licensed or certified business, the court shall either advise the appropriate state or local licensing or certifying authority or shall advise the claimant to do same, but shall retain jurisdiction over the commercial claim.

§1806-A. Trial by jury; how obtained; discretionary costs

A claimant commencing an action upon a commercial claim under this article shall be deemed to have waived a trial by jury, but if said action shall be removed to a regular part of the court, the claimant shall have the same right to demand a trial by jury as if such action had originally been begun in such part. Any party to such action, other than the claimant, prior to the day upon which he is notified to appear or answer, may file with the court a demand for a trial by jury and his affidavit that there are issues of fact in the action requiring such a trial, specifying the same and stating that such trial is desired and intended in good faith. Such demand and affidavit shall be accompanied with the jury fee required by law and an undertaking in the sum of fifty dollars in such form as may be approved by the rules, payable to the other party or parties, conditioned upon the payment of any costs which may be entered against him in the said action or any appeal within thirty days after the entry thereof; or, in lieu of said undertaking, the sum of fifty dollars may be deposited with the clerk of the court and thereupon the clerk shall forthwith transmit such original papers or duly attested copies thereof as may be provided by the rules to the part of the court to which the action shall have been transferred and assigned and such part may require pleadings in such action as though it had been begun by the service of a summons. Such action may be considered a preferred cause of action. In any commercial claim which may have been transferred to another part of the court, the court may award costs up to twenty-five dollars to the claimant if the claimant prevails.

§1807-A. Proceedings on default and review of judgments

(a) A claimant commencing an action upon a commercial claim under this article shall be deemed to have waived all right to appeal, except that either party may appeal on the sole grounds that substantial justice has not been done between the parties according to the rules and principles of substantive law.

(b) The clerk shall mail notice of the default judgment by first class mail, both to the claimant and to the party complained against. Such notice shall inform the defaulting party, in language promulgated by the state office of court administration, of such party's legal obligation to pay; that failure to pay may result in garnishments, repossessions, seizures and similar actions; and that if there was a reasonable excuse for the default the defaulting party may apply to have the default vacated by submitting a written request to the court.

(c) Proceedings on default under this article are to be governed by, but are not limited to, section five thousand fifteen of the civil practice law and rules.

§1808-A. Judgment obtained to be res judicata in certain cases

A judgment obtained under this article may be pleaded as res judicata only as to the amount involved in the particular action and shall not otherwise be deemed an adjudication of any fact at issue or found therein in any other action or court.

§1809-A. Procedures relating to corporations, associations, insurers and assignees

(a) Any corporation, including a municipal corporation or public benefit corporation, partnership, or association, which has its principal office in the state of New York and an assignee of any commercial claim may institute an action or proceeding under this article.

(b) No person or co-partnership, engaged directly or indirectly in the business of collection and adjustment of claims, and no corporation or association, directly or indirectly, itself or by or through its officers, agents or employees, shall solicit, buy or take an assignment of, or be in any manner interested in buying or taking an assignment of a bond, promissory note, bill of exchange, book debt, or other thing in action, or any claim or demand, with the intent and for purpose of bringing an action or proceeding thereon under this article.

(c) A corporation, partnership or association, which institutes an action or proceeding under this article shall be limited to five such actions or proceedings per calendar month. Such corporation, partnership or association shall complete and file with the clerk the required certification, provided it is true and verified as to its truthfulness, as a prerequisite to the institution of an action or proceeding in this part of the court.

(d) A corporation may appear as a party in any action brought pursuant to this article by an attorney as well as by any authorized officer, director or employee of the corporation provided that the appearance by a non-lawyer on behalf of a corporation shall be deemed to constitute the requisite authority to bind the corporation in a settlement or trial. The court or arbitrator may make reasonable inquiry to determine the authority of any person who appears for the corporation in a commercial claims part case.

§1810-A. Limitation on right to resort to commercial claims procedures

If the clerk shall find that the procedures of the commercial claims part are sought to be utilized by a claimant for purposes of oppression or harassment, as where a claimant has previously resorted to such procedures on the same claim and has been unsuccessful after the hearing thereon, the clerk may in his discretion compel the claimant to make application to the court for leave to prosecute the claim in the commercial claim part. The court upon such application may inquire into the circumstances and, if it shall find that the claim has already been adjudicated, or that the claim is sought to be brought on solely for purposes of oppression or harassment and not under color of right, it may make an order denying the claimant the use of the commercial claims part to prosecute the claim.

§1811-A. Indexing commercial claims part judgments

All wholly or partially unsatisfied commercial claims part judgments shall be indexed alphabetically and chronologically under the name of the defendant. Upon satisfying the judgment, the defendant shall present appropriate proof to the court and the court shall indicate such in the records.

§1812-A. Enforcement of commercial claims judgments

Where a judgment has been entered in a commercial claims part and remains unsatisfied, the commercial claims clerk shall, upon request, issue information subpoenas, at nominal cost, for the judgment creditor and provide the creditor with assistance on their preparation and use.

§1813-A. Duty to pay judgments

(a) Any person, partnership, firm or corporation which is sued a commercial claims part for any cause of action arising out of business activities, shall pay any judgment rendered against it in true name or in any name in which it conducts business. "True name" includes the legal name of a natural person and the name under which a partnership, firm or corporation is licensed, registered,

incorporated or otherwise authorized to do business. "Conducting business" as used in this section shall include, but not limited to, maintaining signs at business premises or on business sales slips, checks, invoices or receipts. Whenever a judgment has been rendered against a person, partnership, firm or corporation other than its true name and the judgment has remained unpaid thirty-five days after receipt by the judgment debtor of notice of entry, the aggrieved judgment creditor shall be entitled to commence an action in commercial claims part against such judgment debtor, notwithstanding the jurisdictional limit of the court, for the sum of the original judgment, costs, reasonable attorney's fees, and one hundred dollars.

(b) Whenever a judgment which relates to activities for which a license is required has been rendered against a business which is licensed by a state or local licensing authority and which remains unpaid for thirty-five days after receipt by the judgment debtor of notice of it entry and the judgment has not been stayed or appealed, the state or local licensing authority shall consider such failure to pay, if deliberate or part of a pattern of similar conduct indicating recklessness, as a basis for the revocation, suspension, conditioning or refusal to grant or renew such license. Nothing herein shall be construed to preempt an authority's existing policy if it is more restrictive.

(c) The clerk shall attach to the notice of suit required under this article a notice of the duty imposed by this section.

§1814-A. Designation of defendant; amendment procedure

(a) A party who is ignorant, in whole or in part, of the true name of a person, partnership, firm or corporation which may properly be made a party defendant, may proceed against such defendant in any name used by the person, partnership, firm or corporation in conducting business, as defined in subdivision (a) of section eighteen hundred thirteen-A of this article.

(b) If the true name of the defendant becomes known at any time prior to the hearing on the merits, such information shall be brought to the attention of the clerk, who shall immediately amend all prior proceedings and papers. The clerk shall send an amended notice to the defendant, without payment of additional fees by the plaintiff, and all subsequent proceedings and papers shall be amended accordingly.

(c) In every action in the commercial claims part, at the hearing on the merits, the judge or arbitrator shall determine the defendant's true name. The clerk shall amend all prior proceedings and papers to conform to such determination, and all subsequent proceedings and papers shall be amended accordingly.

(d) A party against whom a judgment has been entered pursuant to this article, in any proceeding under section five thousand fifteen of the civil practice law and rules for relief from such judgment, shall disclose its true name; any and all names in which it is conducting business; and any and all names in which it was conducting business at the time of the transaction or occurrence on which such judgment is based. All subsequent proceedings and papers shall be amended to conform to such disclosure.

APPENDIX B
FORMS

The forms on the following pages are explained throughout the book. Some counties have their own forms. If forms are available in your county, then you should use those forms. Judges and court clerks are more comfortable using forms that they have used before. But if your county does not provide forms, or if your type of claim is not covered by an available form, then use the forms in this book.

(Example of the application you will be required to complete to start your claim)

THIS APPLICATION TO FILE CLAIM BECOMES PUBLIC RECORD

Return to: Small Claim_____
(Name of your court)   Commercial Claim _____
                     Consumer Transaction _____

NAME OF CLAIMANT _____ DAYTIME PHONE _____
           (Name of Person or company filing claim)
ARE YOU A PARTNERSHIP OR A CORPORATION (yes) _____   **(no)** _____
ADDRESS _____ CITY_____ ZIP_____
NAME OF DEFENDANT_____ DAYTIME PHONE _____
           (Name of person or company you are filing against)
ADDRESS _____ CITY_____ZIP_____
AMOUNT OF CLAIM $_____ (do not include filing fee) DATE CLAIM AROSE _____
NATURE OF CLAIM (The reason you are filing claim) **PLEASE KEEP UNDER 25 WORDS**

_____
_____
_____

SIGNATURE OF CLAIMANT_____ TODAY'S DATE_____
THIS SECTION MUST BE COMPLETED AND NOTARIZED FOR A COMMERCIAL CLAIM
I HEREBY CERTIFY THAT NO MORE THAN FIVE (5) ACTIONS OR PROCEEDINGS (INCLUDING THE INSTANT ACTION OR PROCEEDING) HAVE BEEN INITIATED IN THE COURTS OF THIS STATE DURING THE PRESENT CALENDAR MONTH.

_____   _____
(Signature of Claimant)   (Signature of Notary/Clerk/Judge)
ADDRESS OF PRINCIPAL OFFICE (Must be in the State of New York)
_____ CITY _____ ZIP _____
Note: The Commercial Claims Part shall have no jurisdiction over and shall dismiss any case where this certification is not made.
COMPLETE THIS SECTION FOR COMMERCIAL CLAIMS ARISING OUT OF A CONSUMER TRANSACTION
I HEREBY CERTIFY THAT I HAVE MAILED A DEMAND LETTER BY ORDINARY FIRST CLASS MAIL TO THE PARTY COMPLAINED AGAINST, NO LESS THAT TEN (10) DAYS AND NO MORE THAT ONE HUNDRED EIGHTY (180) DAYS BEFORE I COMMENCED THIS CLAIM.
I HEREBY CERTIFY, BASED UPON INFORMATION AND BELIEF, THAT NO MORE THAT FIVE (5) ACTIONS OR PROCEEDINGS (INCLUDING THE INSTANT ACTION OR PROCEEDING) PURSUANT TO THE COMMERCIAL CLAIMS PROCEDURE HAVE BEEN INITIATED IN THE COURTS OF THIS STATE DURING THE PRESENT CALENDAR MONTH.

_____   _____
(Signature of Claimant)   (Signature of Notary/Clerk/Judge)
Note: The Commercial claims Part will not allow your action to proceed if this certification is not made and properly completed.
FILING FEE: SMALL CLAIM $10.00 for claims $1,000.00 and less, $15.00 for claims over $1,000.00—COMMERCIAL CLAIM $22.84, CONSUMER TRANSACTION $22.84

COMMERCIAL CLAIM ARISING OUT OF CONSUMER TRANSACTION
DEMAND LETTER

DATE:

TO: _____

            (Name of Defendant)

      _____

      _____

      _____

            (Address)

Please take notice that you have failed to pay a debt owed to _____ which you incurred on _____, _____. The amount remaining unpaid on the debt is $ _____.

Demand is hereby made that this money be paid. Unless payment of this amount is received by the undersigned not later than _____, _____ a lawsuit will be brought against you in the commercial claims part of the court.

If a lawsuit is brought, you will be notified of the hearing date, and you will be entitled to appear at the hearing and present any defense you may have to this claim.

(IF APPLICABLE) Our records show that you have made the following payment(s) in partial satisfaction of this debt:

(Fill in dates and amounts paid)   _____

                                        _____

                                        _____

A copy of the original debut instrument - your agreement to pay - is attached. The names and addresses of the parties to that original debt agreement are :

         _____

         _____

         _____

         _____

(To be completed if the claimant was not a party to the original transaction)

              _____

              _____

              _____

             (Typed or printed name & address of claimant)

(This is an example of the type of notice that a defendant is required to receive)

(Name of Court)
TO: _____

    Take Notice that _____ asks judgment in this Court against you for $ ____ together with costs, upon the following claim:_____

_____

_____

    There will be a hearing before the Court upon this claim on _____, _____, at _____ o'clock __M in the Small Claims Part, held at _____.

    You must appear and present your defense and any counterclaim you may desire to assert at the hearing at the time and place above set forth (a corporation must be represented by an attorney or any authorized officer, director or employee). **IF YOU DO NOT APPEAR, JUDGMENT WILL BE ENTERED AGAINST YOU BY DEFAULT EVEN THOUGH YOU MAY HAVE A VALID DEFENSE.** If your defense or counterclaim, if any, is supported by witnesses, account books, receipts or other documents, you must produce them at the hearing. The Clerk, if requested, will issue subpoenas for witnesses, without fee therefor.

    If you admit the claim, but desire time to pay, you must appear personally on the day set for the hearing and state to the Court your reasons for desiring time to pay.

Dated: _____, _____.

                                     _____
                                               Clerk

NOTE: If you desire a jury trial, you must, before the day upon which you have been notified to appear, file with the Clerk of the Court a written demand for a trial by jury. You must also pay to the clerk a jury fee of $55 and file an undertaking in the sum of $50, or deposit such sum in cash to secure the payment of any costs that may be awarded against you. You will also be required to make an affidavit specifying the issues of fact which you desire to have tried by a jury and stating that such trial is desired and demanded in good faith.

    Under the law, the Court may award $25 additional costs to the plaintiff if a jury trial is demanded by you and a decision is rendered against you.

_____(Name of Court)

STATE OF NEW YORK: COUNTY OF _____

SMALL CLAIMS PART

_____

_____

_____ }

          Plaintiff, }   **Demand for Jury Trial**

                }

  against }

               }

_____ Defendant. }

_____}

      PLEASE TAKE NOTICE that _____, defendant hereby demands a trial by jury in the above captioned matter.

Dated _____, _____

_____(signature)

_____(address)

_____

_____(telephone)

_____(Name of Court)
STATE OF NEW YORK: COUNTY OF _____
SMALL CLAIMS PART

_____

_____ Plaintiff,	} } } }	**Affidavit**
against	}	
_____ Defendant.	} } }	

_____, being sworn, deposes and says::

I. I am the defendant in the above captioned matter.

II. This action was commenced on _____, _____.

III. There are issues of fact in this action which require a jury trial. The issues of fact requiring a jury trial are the following.
1. _____
_____
_____
_____
_____
_____
_____
_____
_____
_____
_____

IV. Defendant's demand for a trial by jury is desired and intended in good faith.

_____(Signature)

Sworn to me on
This ____day of _____, _____

_____(notary)

My commission expires _____.

Notice of claim for Personal Injury

TO:_____*(Name of attorney representing county, city, town, or village)*

    PLEASE TAKE NOTICE that I, _____, the claimant herein, hereby makes a claim for negligence against the _____,*(Name of county, city, town, or village)* and that an action will be commenced to recover pursuant to law.

    The claimant herein resides at _____, county of _____, state of New York.

    The injury for which this claim is made occurred on the _____ day of _____, _____, at _____,*(identify place where injury occurred)* and was caused when _____ _____ _____.*(state manner in which claim arose)* Said injury was sustained wholly through the negligence of _____ _____.

(name of county, city, town, or village)

    As a result of said negligence, the claimant has suffered the following personal injury.

_____

_____

(detail injuries)

                        _____

                                Claimant

Sworn to me on
This ____day of _____, _____

_____(notary)

My commission expires _____.

Notice of Claim for Property Damage

TO:_____*(Name of attorney representing county, city, town, or village)*

PLEASE TAKE NOTICE that I, _____, the claimant herein, hereby makes a claim for negligence against the _____,*(Name of county, city, town, or village)* and that an action will be commenced to recover pursuant to law.

The claimant herein resides at _____, county of _____, state of New York.

The property damage for which this claim is made occurred on the _____ day of _____, _____, at _____,*(identify place where injury occurred)* and was caused when _____ _____ _____.*(state manner in which claim arose)* Said property damage was sustained wholly through the negligence of _____.

(name of county, city, town, or village)

As a result of said negligence, the claimant has suffered the following property damage.

_____ _____

(detail damages)

_____

Claimant

Sworn to me on
This _____day of _____, _____

_____(notary)

My commission expires _____.

Promissory Note

For value received, I, _____, of
_____(address), _____ (city),
_____ County, _____ (state), promise to pay
_____ Dollars ($_____) to the order of
_____ (Payee), of _____
(address), _____ (city), _____County, and
_____ (state) on _____ (date) with interest
thereon at the rate of _____ percent (_____%) annually.

_____

Signature of Maker

_____(Name of Court)

STATE OF NEW YORK: COUNTY OF _____

SMALL CLAIMS PART

_____

_____

_____   }

            Plaintiff,   }   **SUBPOENA**

                        }

  against   }

                        }

_____ Defendant.   }

_____}

TO:

     YOU ARE HEREBY COMMANDED to appear before the Honorable _____, one of the Judges of our said court, at _____, New York, on _____, _____, at _____M., in the above captioned cause. If you fail to appear, you may be in contempt of court.

     WITNESS, _____, as Clerk of the _____, and the seal of said Court, at the Courthouse at _____, New York.

_____
Date

(SEAL)

_____
Clerk of the Court

_____

Plaintiff/Defendant
Address:

_____(Name of Court)

STATE OF NEW YORK: COUNTY OF _____

SMALL CLAIMS PART

_____

_____

_____   }
                    Plaintiff,   }   **SUBPOENA DUCES**
                                                    }   **TECUM**
                                                    }
    against   }
                                                    }
_____   Defendant.   }
_____}

TO:

     YOU ARE HEREBY COMMANDED to appear before the Honorable _____, one of the Judges of our said Court, at _____, New York, on _____, _____, at _____M., to testify and give evidence in the above styled cause and to have with you at said time and place the following:

If you fail to appear, you will be deemed guilty of contempt of court, and liable to pay all loss and damage sustained thereby to the party aggrieved, and forfeit $50 in addition thereto.

    WITNESS my hand and seal of said Court on _____, _____.

                               _____

                               CLERK OF THE COURT

(SEAL)

_____(Name of Court)

STATE OF NEW YORK: COUNTY OF _____

SMALL CLAIMS PART

_____

_____

_____		}
Plaintiff,		}
		} **Affidavit of Service of**
		} **Subpoena**
against		}
		}
_____ Defendant.		}
_____		}

_____being duly sworn, deposes and says: that deponent is not a party to this action, is over 18 years of age and resides at _____. That on _____, _____, deponent served the annexed subpoena upon _____, the person to whom said subpoena is directed, by then and there delivering to and leaving with him a copy of said subpoena, and by paying to him at the same time and place _____dollars as and for his fees for mileage and for one day's attendant as such witness.

The person served was [insert description of the person served including his or her sex, color of skin, hair color, approximate age, approximate weight and height, and other identifying features]
_____
_____

_____(signature of deponent)
(Type name of deponent)

Sworn to me on
This _____day of _____, _____
_____(notary)
My commission expires _____.

STATE OF NEW YORK
COUNTY OF _____
TOWN OF _____

_____

Plaintiff - Judgment Creditor

v.   **INFORMATION SUBPOENA**
                                            (Small Claims)

Defendant - Judgment Debtor

_____

THE PEOPLE OF THE STATE OF NEW YORK
TO (Judgment Debtor) _____
Address:

      WHEREAS, in the above entitled action in the small claims court of the Town Court of the Town of _____, a judgment was entered on _____, _____ in favor of the judgment creditor and against the judgment debtor in the amount of $_____ which sum together with interest thereon from the date of said judgment remains due and unpaid:

      NOW, WHEREFORE WE COMMAND YOU, that you answer in writing under oath, separately and fully, each question in the questionnaire accompanying this subpoena, each answer referring to the question to which it responds; and that you return the answers together with the original of the questions within 7 days after your receipt of the questions and this subpoena in the prepaid addressed return envelope enclosed.

      TAKE NOTICE that false swearing or failure to comply with this subpoena is punishable as a contempt of court.

_____

HON.
Town Court of the Town of _____
Mailing Address:

Enclosed: Question form; original and copy.
     Prepaid, addressed return envelope

AFFIDAVIT OF SERVICE BY MAIL

STATE OF NEW YORK: COUNTY OF :_____:ss.:

_____ being duly sworn, says: that deponent is not a part to this action, is over 18 years of age and resides at _____

_____;

That on _____, _____ deponent served the within subpoena on the judgment debtor by mailing a copy of same, accompanied by a copy and original of written questions, a prepaid addressed return envelope in a securely sealed postpaid wrapper properly addressed to _____ at _____.

Strike out (a) or (b):

(a) by registered mail, return receipt requested. Deponent delivered said wrapper to the Registry Clerk at the post office and paid the requisite fee. Return Receipt No. _____ is attached hereto.

(b) by certified mail, return receipt requested. Deponent delivered said wrapper with the requisite postage and return receipt card affixed, in (a post office) (official depository under the care and custody of the United States Postal Service) within the State of New York. Return Receipt No. _____ is attached hereto.

_____

Print name beneath signature

Sworn to before me on

_____, _____.

Notary Public

QUESTIONS AND ANSWERS MADE IN RESPONSE TO THE WITHIN SUBPOENA

Q.   What is your name and address?

A.

Q.   Please state.   (i) whether the witness has any property, or property in which the judgment debtor has an interest, in its possession, custody, or control; (ii) whether it is indebted to the judgment debtor and whether such debt is due or to become due; (iii) whether it has within the past year had financial, business, or other relations with the judgment debtor either individually or as an agent, employee, trustee, officer, director, or partner of another, describing fully any such property, interest, debt, or relationship.

A.

_____

Sworn to me on

This _____ day of _____, _____
_____ (Notary)
My commission expires _____

COUNTY COURT, _____ COUNTY, NEW YORK
SMALL CLAIMS DIVISION
CASE NO._____

_____
_____
PLAINTIFF(S)

Address:

VS.

_____
_____
DEFENDANT(S)

Address:

SATISFACTION OF JUDGMENT

    Plaintiff(s) _____, holders of a judgment
in the above-styled cause, which judgment was rendered on _____, _____
against _____ in the amount of
_____ dollars ($_____), and recorded in Official
Records Books _____ Page _____, Public Records of _____
County, New York, hereby acknowledge full payment and satisfaction of said judgment, and hereby
consent that said judgment shall be satisfied of record.

_____

_____

    Sworn to and subscribed before me by _____
who is personally known to me or produced _____ as
identification this _____ day of _____, _____.

_____
Notary Public
State of New York
My commission expires_____

_____(Name of Court)

STATE OF NEW YORK: COUNTY OF _____

SMALL CLAIMS PART

_____

_____

_____   }

           Plaintiff,   }

                                 }

  against   }

                                 }

_____   Defendant.   }

_____}

MOTION TO SET ASIDE DEFAULT AND DEFAULT JUDGMENT

Comes now _____ Defendant, in the above-styled cause, and respectfully requests that this Honorable Court set aside the Default and Default Judgment entered in this cause on the _____ day of _____, _____.

I did not appear because:

_____

_____

_____

WHEREFORE, Defendant moves this Honorable Court for an Order setting aside the Default and Default Judgment previously entered.

_____   _____

Defendant's Signature   _____

                                       Defendant's Address and telephone number

STATE OF NEW YORK
COUNTY OF _____
TOWN OF _____

_____
                                        Plaintiff,

          v.   **NOTICE OF APPEAL**
                                                                    (small claims)

                              Defendant.

_____

SIRS:
          PLEASE TAKE NOTICE that I, the undersigned _____
(plaintiff) _____ (defendant) hereby appeal to the County Court of
_____ County from a judgment entered against me in the above entitled
action on the _____ day of _____, _____ in the Small Claims Part of the
above Town Court (granting) (denying) damages claimed by plaintiff for $ _____
in that substantial justice has not been done between the parties according to the rules and principles of substantive law.
DATED: _____, _____.

                                             _____

                                             plaintiff
                                             _____

                                             _____
                                             address

                                             _____
                                             telephone number

                                             _____

                                             defendant
                                             _____

                                             _____
                                             address

                                             _____
                                             telephone number

TO: *Clerk of Town Court
*Adverse party

*Must be filed within 30 days from date of entry of Judgment by trial court

STATE OF NEW YORK:
SUPREME COURT   COUNTY OF _____

_____

_____, }
                    Plaintiff,   }   **Execution against property**
                                      }   Index No. _____
                                      }
   against   }
                                      }
_____, Defendant.   }
_____}

THE PEOPLE OF THE STATE OF NEW YORK
TO THE SHERIFF OF THE COUNTY OF _____
GREETING:
        WHEREAS, judgment was entered on _____, _____, in an action
in the _____ Court, County of _____, in favor of
_____, plaintiff, and against
_____, defendant, whose last known address is
_____, County of _____, State of New York,
for the sum of _____ ($_____) Dollars, and whereas the sum of
_____ ($_____) Dollars with interest thereon from the date of entry of
judgment is now due thereon.
        WHEREAS, a transcript of the judgment was filed on the _____ day of
_____, with the Clerk of the County of _____, in which County
the judgment was entered.
        WE DIRECT that you satisfy the judgment out of the real and personal property of the judg-
ment debtor, _____, and the debts due to _____,
and that only the property in which the judgment debtor who is not deceased, has an interest, or the
debts owed to the judgment debtor, shall be levied upon or sold thereunder, and to return this execution to the clerk of this court within sixty days after issuance unless service of this execution is
made in accordance with CPLR 5231 or 5232(a), or within extensions of that time made in writing
by the judgment creditor.

        Dated _____   _____
                                                         Clerk of the Court

STATE OF NEW YORK:

SUPREME COURT   COUNTY OF _____

_____

_____,

               Plaintiff,   }

                                   }

     against   }

                                   }

_____,   Defendant.   }

_____}

Execution against income
Index No. _____

THE PEOPLE OF THE STATE OF NEW YORK
TO THE SHERIFF OF THE COUNTY OF _____
GREETING:
     WHEREAS, judgment was entered on _____, _____, in an action in the _____ Court, County of _____, in favor of _____, plaintiff, and against _____ _____, defendant, whose last known address is _____, County of _____, State of New York, for the sum of _____ ($_____) Dollars, and whereas the sum of _____ ($_____) Dollars with interest thereon from the date of entry of judgment is now due thereon.

     WHEREAS, a transcript of the judgment was filed on the _____ day of _____, with the Clerk of the County of _____, in which County the judgment was entered.

     Whereas _____, the judgment debtor, will receive or is receiving from _____, the sum of _____ ($_____) dollars weekly, you are directed to collect in installments from each weekly payment aforesaid the sum of _____ dollars.

THIS INCOME EXECUTION DIRECTS THE WITHHOLDING OF UP TO TEN PERCENT OF THE JUDGMENTS DEBTOR'S GROSS INCOME. IN CERTAIN CASES, HOWEVER, STATE OF FEDERAL LAW DOES NOT PERMIT THE WITHHOLDING OF THE MUCH OF THE JUDGMENT DEBTOR'S GROSS INCOME. THE JUDGMENT DEBTOR IS REFERRED TO NEW YORK CIVIL PRACTICE LAW AND RULES §5231 AND 15 UNITED STATES CODE §1671 ET. SEQ.

I. LIMITATIONS ON THE AMOUNT THAT CAN BE WITHHELD.

A. AN INCOME EXECUTION FOR INSTALLMENTS FROM A JUDGMENT DEBTOR'S GROSS INCOME CANNOT EXCEED TEN PERCENT (10%) OF THE JUDGMENT DEBTOR'S GROSS INCOME.

B. IF A JUDGMENT DEBTOR'S WEEKLY DISPOSABLE EARNING ARE LESS THAN THIRTY (30) TIME THE CURRENT FEDERAL MINIMUM WAGE (, PER HOUR), OR ( ) NO DEDUCTION CAN BE MADE FROM THE JUDGMENT DEBTOR'S EARNINGS UNDER THIS INCOME EXECUTION.

C. A JUDGMENT DEBTOR'S WEEKLY DISPOSABLE EARNINGS CANNOT BE REDUCED BELOW THE AMOUNT ARRIVED AT BY MULTIPLYING THIRTY (30) TIME THE CURRENT FEDERAL MINIMUM WAGE ($, PER HOUR), OR ($), UNDER THIS INCOME EXECUTION.

D. IF DEDUCTIONS ARE BEING MAD FROM A JUDGMENT DEBTOR'S EARNINGS UNDER ANY ORDER FOR ALIMONY, SUPPORT OR MAINTENANCE FOR FAMILY MEMBERS OR FORMER SPOUSES, AND THOSE DEDUCTIONS EQUAL OR EXCEED TWENTY-FIVE PERCENT (25%) OF THE JUDGMENT DEBTOR'S DISPOSABLE EARNINGS, NO DEDUCTION CAN BE MADE FROM THE JUDGMENT DEBTOR'S EARNINGS UNDER THIS INCOME EXECUTION.

E. IF DEDUCTIONS ARE BEING MADE FROM A JUDGEMENT DEBTOR'S EARNINGS UNDER ANY ORDERS FOR ALIMONY SUPPORT OR MAINTENANCE FOR FAMILY MEMBERS OR FORMER SPOUSE, AND THOSE DEDUCTIONS ARE LESS THAN TWENTY-FIVE PERCENT (25%) OF THE JUDGMENT DEBTOR'S DISPOSABLE EARNINGS, DEDUCTIONS MAY BE MADE FROM THE JUDGMENT DEBTOR'S EARNING UNDER THIS INCOME EXECUTION. HOWEVER, THE AMOUNT ARRIVED AT BY ADDING THE DEDUCTIONS FROM EARNING MADE UNDER THIS EXECUTION TO THE DEDUCTIONS MADE FROM EARNINGS UNDER ANY ORDERS FOR ALIMONY, SUPPORT OR MAINTENANCE FOR FAMILY MEMBERS OR FORMER SPOUSES CANNOT EXCEED TWENTY-FIVE PERCENT (25%) OF THE JUDGMENT DEBTOR'S DISPOSABLE EARNINGS.

NOTE: NOTHING IN THIS NOTICE LIMITS THE PROPORTION OR AMOUNT WHICH MAY BE DEDUCTED UNDER ANY ORDER FOR ALIMONY, SUPPORT OR MAINTENANCE FOR FAMILY MEMBERS OR FORMER SPOUSES.

II. EXPLANATION OF LIMITATIONS

DEFINITIONS:

DISPOSABLE EARNINGS

DISPOSABLE EARNINGS ARE THAT PART OF AN INDIVIDUAL'S EARNINGS LEFT AFTER DEDUCTING THOSE AMOUNTS THAT ARE REQUIRED BY LAW TO BE WITHHELD (FOR EXAMPLE, TAXES, SOCIAL SECURITY, AND UNEMPLOYMENT INSURANCE, BUT NO DEDUCTIONS FOR UNION DUES, INSURANCE PLANS, ETC.).

GROSS INCOME

GROSS INCOME IS SALARY, WAGES OR OTHER INCOME, INCLUDING ANY AND ALL OVERTIME EARNINGS, COMMISSIONS, AND INCOME FROM TRUSTS, BEFORE ANY DEDUCTIONS ARE MADE FROM SUCH INCOME.

ILLUSTRATIONS REGARDING EARNINGS:

IF DISPOSABLE EARNINGS IS: AMOUNT TO PAY OR DEDUCT UNDER THIS INCOME EXECUTION IS:

(a) 30 TIMES FEDERAL
MINIMUM WAGE ($)
OR LESS

(b) MORE THAN 30 TIMES
FEDERAL MINIMUM
WAGE ($) AND LESS
THAN 40 TIMES FEDERAL
MINIMUM WAGE ($)

THE LESSER OF: THE EXCESS
OVER 30 TIMES THE FEDERAL
MINIMUM WAGE ($) IN
DISPOSABLE EARNINGS,
OR 10% OF GROSS EARNINGS

(c) 40 TIMES THE FEDERAL
MINIMUM WAGE ($)
OR MORE

THE LESSER OF: 25% OF
DISPOSABLE EARNING OR 10%
OF GROSS EARNINGS.

III. NOTICE: YOU MAY BE ABLE TO CHALLENGE THIS INCOME EXECUTION THROUGH THE PROCEDURES PROVIDED IN CPLR §5231(I) AND CPLR §5240 IF YOU THINK THAT THE AMOUNT OF YOUR INCOME BEING DEDUCTED UNDER THIS INCOME EXECUTION EXCEEDS THE AMOUNT PERMITTED BY STATE OR FEDERAL LAW, YOU SHOULD ACT PROMPTLY BECAUSE THE MONEY WILL BE APPLIED TO THE JUDGMENT IF YOU CLAIM THAT THE AMOUNT OF YOUR INCOME BEING DEDUCTED UNDER THIS INCOME EXECUTION EXCEEDS THE AMOUNT PERMITTED BY STATE OR FEDERAL LAW, YOU SHOULD CONTACT YOUR EMPLOYER OR OTHER PERSON PAYING YOUR INCOME. FURTHER, YOU MAY CONSULT AN ATTORNEY, INCLUDING LEGAL AID IF YOU QUALIFY. NEW YORK STATE LAW PROVIDES TWO PROCE-DURES THROUGH WHICH AN INCOME EXECUTION CAN BE CHALLENGED.

CPLR §5231(I) MODIFICATION. AT ANY TIME, THE JUDGMENT DEBTOR MAY MAKE A MOTION TO A COURT FOR AN ORDER MODIFYING AN INCOME EXECUTION.

CPLR §5240 MODIFICATION OR PROTECTIVE ORDER: SUPERVISION OR ENFORCEMENT. AT ANY TIME, THE JUDGMENT DEBTOR MAY MAKE A MOTION TO A COURT FOR AN ORDER DENYING, LIMITING, CONDITIONING, REGULATING, EXTENDING OR MODIFYING THE USE OF ANY POST-JUDGMENT ENFORCEMENT PROCEDURE, INCLUDING THE USE OF INCOME EXECUTIONS.

TO THE JUDGMENT DEBTOR:

PLEASE TAKE NOTICE THAT YOU SHALL COMMENCE PAYMENT OF THE INSTALL-MENTS ABOVE MENTIONED TO THE ABOVE NAMED SHERIFF FORTHWITH, AND THAT UPON YOUR DEFAULT, THIS EXECUTION WILL BE SERVED UPON _____, of _____, New York.

Dated _____   _____

                                                    Clerk

INDEX

Your #1 Source for Real World Legal Information...

LEGAL SURVIVAL GUIDES™

- Written by lawyers
- Simple English explanation of the law
- Forms and instructions included

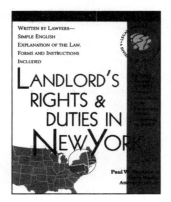  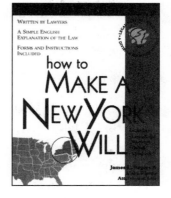

LANDLORD'S RIGHTS & DUTIES IN NEW YORK

The perfect resource for any residential or commercial landlord, including: security deposits, evictions, maintenance duties, violations by tenants, and more. This book will help landlords avoid unnecessary legal fees. It explains New York State's extensive landlord/tenant laws.

176 pages; $19.95;
ISBN 1-57071-186-0

HOW TO START A BUSINESS IN NEW YORK

A small business guide that explains the many government regulations for New Yorker's. This book includes information on licensing, labor laws, name registration, sales tax collection, regulatory laws, trademarks, advertising rules, and much more. State and federal forms are included.

192 pages; $16.95;
ISBN 1-57071-185-2

HOW TO MAKE A NEW YORK WILL

This simple guide includes ready-to-use forms and instructions that cover many issues, such as: inheritance laws, joint property, guardianship of your children, living will, and anatomical gifts. It's easy to make your own will without the hassle of a lawyer.

128 pages; $12.95;
ISBN 1-57071-183-6

What our customers say about our books:

"It couldn't be more clear for the lay person." —R.D.

"I want you to know I really appreciate your book. It has saved me a lot of time and money." —L.T.

"Your real estate contracts book has saved me nearly $12,000.00 in closing costs over the past year." —A.B.

"...many of the legal questions that I have had over the years were answered clearly and concisely through your plain English interpretation of the law." —C.E.H.

"If there weren't people out there like you I'd be lost. You have the best books of this type out there." —S.B.

"...your forms and directions are easy to follow." —C.V.M.

Legal Survival Guides are directly available from the publisher, or from your local bookstores.
For credit card orders call 1–800–43–BRIGHT, write P.O. Box 372, Naperville, IL 60566,
or fax 630-961-2168

LEGAL SURVIVAL GUIDES™ NATIONAL TITLES
Valid in All 50 States

LEGAL SURVIVAL IN BUSINESS

How to Form Your Own Corporation (2E)	$19.95
How to Register Your Own Copyright (2E)	$19.95
How to Register Your Own Trademark (2E)	$19.95
Most Valuable Business Forms You'll Ever Need	$19.95
Most Valuable Corporate Forms You'll Ever Need	$24.95
Software Law (with diskette)	$29.95

LEGAL SURVIVAL IN COURT

Crime Victim's Guide to Justice	$19.95
Debtors' Rights (2E)	$12.95
Defend Yourself Against Criminal Charges	$19.95
Grandparents' Rights	$19.95
Help Your Lawyer Win Your Case	$12.95
Jurors' Rights	$9.95
Legal Malpractice and Other Claims Against Your Lawyer	$18.95
Legal Research Made Easy	$14.95
Simple Ways to Protect Yourself From Lawsuits	$24.95
Victim's Rights	$12.95
Winning Your Personal Injury Claim	$19.95

LEGAL SURVIVAL IN REAL ESTATE

How to Buy a Condominium or Townhome	$16.95
How to Negotiate Real Estate Contracts (2E)	$16.95
How to Negotiate Real Estate Leases (2E)	$16.95
Successful Real Estate Brokerage Management	$19.95

LEGAL SURVIVAL IN PERSONAL AFFAIRS

How to File Your Own Bankruptcy (4E)	$19.95
How to File Your Own Divorce (3E)	$19.95
How to Make Your Own Will	$12.95
How to Write Your Own Living Will	$9.95
Living Trusts and Simple Ways to Avoid Probate	$19.95
Neighbor vs. Neighbor	$12.95
Power of Attorney Handbook (2E)	$19.95
Social Security Benefits Handbook	$14.95
U.S.A. Immigration Guide (2E)	$19.95
Guia de Inmigracion a Estados Unidos	$19.95

Legal Survival Guides are directly available from the publisher, or from your local bookstores.

For credit card orders call 1–800–43–BRIGHT, write P.O. Box 372, Naperville, IL 60566, or fax 630-961-2168

LEGAL SURVIVAL GUIDES™ STATE TITLES

Up-to-date for Your State

NEW YORK

How to File for Divorce in NY	$19.95
How to Make a NY Will	$12.95
How to Start a Business in NY	$16.95
How to Win in Small Claims Court in NY	$14.95
Landlord's Rights and Duties in NY	$19.95
New York Power of Attorney Handbook	$12.95

PENNSYLVANIA

How to File for Divorce in PA	$19.95
How to Make a PA Will	$12.95
How to Start a Business in PA	$16.95
Landlord's Rights and Duties in PA	$19.95

FLORIDA

Florida Power of Attorney Handbook	$9.95
How to Change Your Name in FL (3E)	$14.95
How to File a FL Construction Lien (2E)	$19.95
How to File a Guardianship in FL	$19.95
How to File for Divorce in FL (4E)	$21.95
How to Form a Nonprofit Corp in FL (3E)	$19.95
How to Form a Simple Corp in FL (3E)	$19.95
How to Make a FL Will (4E)	$9.95
How to Modify Your FL Divorce Judgement (3E)	$22.95
How to Probate an Estate in FL (2E)	$24.95
How to Start a Business in FL (4E)	$16.95
How to Win in Small Claims Court in FL (5E)	$14.95
Land Trusts in FL (4E)	$24.95
Landlord's Rights and Duties in FL (6E)	$19.95
Women's Legal Rights in FL	$19.95

GEORGIA

How to File for Divorce in GA (2E)	$19.95
How to Make a GA Will (2E)	$9.95
How to Start and Run a GA Business (2E)	$18.95

ILLINOIS

How to File for Divorce in IL	$19.95
How to Make an IL Will	$9.95
How to Start a Business in IL	$16.95

MASSACHUSETTS

How to File for Divorce in MA	$19.95
How to Make a MA Will	$9.95
How to Probate an Estate in MA	$19.95
How to Start a Business in MA	$16.95
Landlord's Rights and Duties in MA	$19.95

MICHIGAN

How to File for Divorce in MI	$19.95
How to Make a MI Will	$9.95
How to Start a Business in MI	$16.95

MINNESOTA

How to File for Divorce in MN	$19.95
How to Form a Simple Corporation in MN	$19.95
How to Make a MN Will	$9.95
How to Start a Business in MN	$16.95

NORTH CAROLINA

How to File for Divorce in NC	$19.95
How to Make a NC Will	$9.95
How to Start a Business in NC	$16.95

TEXAS

How to File for Divorce in TX	$19.95
How to Form a Simple Corporation in TX	$19.95
How to Make a TX Will	$9.95
How to Probate an Estate in TX	$19.95
How to Start a Business in TX	$16.95
How to Win in Small Claims Court in TX	$14.95
Landlord's Rights and Duties in TX	$19.95

Legal Survival Guides are directly available from the publisher, or from your local bookstores.

For credit card orders call 1–800–43–BRIGHT, write P.O. Box 372, Naperville, IL 60566, or fax 630-961-2168

Legal Survival Guides™ • Order Form

BILL TO:	SHIP TO:

Phone #	Terms	F.O.B. Chicago, IL	Ship Date

Charge my: □ VISA   □ Mastercard   □ American Express

□ **Money Order** (no personal checks please)

Credit Card Number   Expiration Date

Qty	ISBN	Title	Retail
		Legal Survival Guides Fall 97 National Frontlist	
	1-57071-223-9	How to File Your Own Bankruptcy (4E)	$19.95
	1-57071-224-7	How to File Your Own Divorce (3E)	$19.95
	1-57071-227-1	How to Form Your Own Corporation (2E)	$19.95
	1-57071-228-X	How to Make Your Own Will	$12.95
	1-57071-225-5	How to Register Your Own Copyright (2E)	$19.95
	1-57071-226-3	How to Register Your Own Trademark (2E)	$19.95
		Fall 97 New York Frontlist	
	1-57071-184-4	How to File for Divorce in NY	$19.95
	1-57071-183-6	How to Make a NY Will	$12.95
	1-57071-185-2	How to Start a Business in NY	$16.95
	1-57071-187-9	How to Win in Small Claims Court in NY	$14.95
	1-57071-186-0	Landlord's Rights and Duties in NY	$19.95
	1-57071-188-7	New York Power of Attorney Handbook	$12.95
		Fall 97 Pennsylvania Frontlist	
	1-57071-177-1	How to File for Divorce in PA	$19.95
	1-57071-176-3	How to Make a PA Will	$12.95
	1-57071-178-X	How to Start a Business in PA	$16.95
	1-57071-179-8	Landlord's Rights and Duties in PA	$19.95
		Legal Survival Guides National Backlist	
	1-57071-166-6	Crime Victim's Guide to Justice	$19.95
	1-57248-023-8	Debtors' Rights (2E)	$12.95
	1-57071-162-3	Defend Yourself Against Criminal Charges	$19.95
	1-57248-001-7	Grandparents' Rights	$19.95
	0-913825-99-9	Guia de Inmigracion a Estados Unidos	$19.95
	1-57248-021-1	Help Your Lawyer Win Your Case	$12.95
	1-57071-164-X	How to Buy a Condominium or Townhome	$16.95
	1-57248-035-1	How to Negotiate Real Estate Contracts (2E)	$16.95
	1-57248-036-X	How to Negotiate Real Estate Leases (2E)	$16.95
	1-57071-167-4	How to Write Your Own Living Will	$9.95
	1-57248-031-9	Jurors' Rights	$9.95
	1-57248-032-7	Legal Malpractice and Other Claims Against Your Lawyer	$18.95
	1-57248-008-4	Legal Research Made Easy	$14.95
	1-57248-019-X	Living Trusts and Simple Ways to Avoid Probate	$19.95
	1-57248-022-X	Most Valuable Business Forms You'll Ever Need	$19.95
	1-57248-007-6	Most Valuable Corporate Forms You'll Ever Need	$24.95
	0-913825-41-7	Neighbor vs. Neighbor	$12.95
	1-57248-044-0	Power of Attorney Handbook (2E)	$19.95
	1-57248-020-3	Simple Ways to Protect Yourself From Lawsuits	$24.95
	1-57248-033-5	Social Security Benefits Handbook	$14.95
	1-57071-163-1	Software Law (w/diskette)	$29.95
	0-913825-86-7	Successful Real Estate Brokerage Mgmt.	$19.95
	1-57248-000-9	U.S.A. Immigration Guide (2E)	$19.95
	0-913825-82-4	Victim's Rights	$12.95
	1-57071-165-8	Winning Your Personal Injury Claim	$19.95
		Florida Backlist	
	0-913825-81-6	Florida Power of Attorney Handbook	$9.95
	1-57248-028-9	How to Change Your Name in FL (3E)	$14.95
	0-913825-84-0	How to File a FL Construction Lien (2E)	$19.95
	0-913825-53-0	How to File a Guardianship in FL	$19.95
	1-57248-046-7	How to File for Divorce in FL (4E)	$21.95

Qty	ISBN	Title	Retail
		Florida Backlist (cont')	
	1-57248-004-1	How to Form a Nonprofit Corp in FL (3E)	$19.95
	0-913825-96-4	How to Form a Simple Corp in FL (3E)	$19.95
	1-57248-027-0	How to Make a FL Will (4E)	$9.95
	1-57248-056-4	How to Modify Your FL Divorce Judgement (3E)	$22.95
	1-57248-003-3	How to Probate an Estate in FL (2E)	$24.95
	1-57248-005-X	How to Start a Business in FL (4E)	$16.95
	0-913825-97-2	How to Win in Small Claims Court in FL (5E)	$14.95
	1-57248-029-7	Land Trusts in FL (4E)	$24.95
	1-57248-057-2	Landlord's Rights and Duties in FL (6E)	$19.95
	0-913825-73-5	Women's Legal Rights in FL	$19.95
		Georgia Backlist	
	1-57248-058-0	How to File for Divorce in GA (2E)	$19.95
	1-57248-047-5	How to Make a GA Will (2E)	$9.95
	1-57248-026-2	How to Start and Run a GA Business (2E)	$18.95
		Illinois Backlist	
	1-57248-042-4	How to File for Divorce in IL	$19.95
	1-57248-043-2	How to Make an IL Will	$9.95
	1-57248-041-6	How to Start a Business in IL	$16.95
		Massachusetts Backlist	
	1-57248-051-3	How to File for Divorce in MA	$19.95
	1-57248-050-5	How to Make a MA Will	$9.95
	1-57248-053-X	How to Probate an Estate in MA	$19.95
	1-57248-054-8	How to Start a Business in MA	$16.95
	1-57248-055-6	Landlord's Rights and Duties in MA	$19.95
		Michigan Backlist	
	1-57248-014-9	How to File for Divorce in MI	$19.95
	1-57248-015-7	How to Make a MI Will	$9.95
	1-57248-013-0	How to Start a Business in MI	$16.95
		Minnesota Backlist	
	1-57248-039-4	How to File for Divorce in MN	$19.95
	1-57248-040-8	How to Form a Simple Corporation in MN	$19.95
	1-57248-037-8	How to Make a MN Will	$9.95
	1-57248-038-6	How to Start a Business in MN	$16.95
		North Carolina Backlist	
	0-913825-94-8	How to File for Divorce in NC	$19.95
	0-913825-92-1	How to Make a NC Will	$9.95
	0-913825-93-X	How to Start a Business in NC	$16.95
		Texas Backlist	
	0-913825-91-3	How to File for Divorce in TX	$19.95
	1-57248-009-2	How to Form a Simple Corporation in TX	$19.95
	0-913825-89-1	How to Make a TX Will	$9.95
	1-57248-010-6	How to Probate an Estate in TX	$19.95
	0-913825-90-5	How to Start a Business in TX	$16.95
	1-57248-012-2	How to Win in Small Claims Court in TX	$14.95
	1-57248-011-4	Landlord's Rights and Duties in TX	$19.95
		SUBTOTAL	
		IL Residents add 6.75%, FL Residents add county sales tax	
		Shipping— $4.00 for 1st book, $1.00 each additional	
		Total	

To order, call Sourcebooks at 1-800-43-BRIGHT or FAX (630)961-2168 (Bookstores, libraries, wholesalers—please call for discount)

347.747 Rogers, James L.,
R   1965-

         How to win in small
         claims court in New
         York.

$14.95   05/11/1998

DATE			

BAKER & TAYLOR